Eucharist and Witness

Eucharist and Witness

Orthodox Perspectives on the Unity and Mission of the Church

Petros Vassiliadis

WCC Publications, Geneva

Holy Cross Orthodox Press,
Brookline, Massachusetts

Cover design: Michael Martin
Cover illustration: Jesus washing the feet of his disciples. Fresco in the nave
of the church of St Paraskevi in Geroskipos, Cyprus, late 15th century. Repro-
duced from *St Metropole of Paphos: History and Art,* by A. Papageorghiou,
Nicosia, 1996.

© 1998 WCC Publications, World Council of Churches,
150 route de Ferney, 1211 Geneva 2, Switzerland

ISBN: 2-8254-1261-9

Holy Cross Orthodox Press, 50 Goddard Avenue,
Brookline, MA 02445, USA
ISBN: 1-885652-21-6

Library of Congress Cataloging-in-Publication Data

Vassiliadis, Petros.
    Eucharist and witness: Orthodox perspectives on the unity and mission of
    the church / Petros Vassiliadis.
        p.,   x   cm.
    Includes bibliographical references (p.   ).
    ISBN 2-8254-1261-9. – ISBN 1-885652-21-6 (paper)
    1. Orthodox Eastern Church–Doctrines. 2. Lord's Supper and Christian
    union. 3. Mission of the church. I. Title
BX323.V38 1998
262'.019–dc21   98-39733
                                                                      CIP

Printed in Switzerland

Table of Contents

Preface

While approaching the jubilee of the WCC, to be celebrated in 1998 in its eighth assembly in Harare, Zimbabwe, it is quite important for member churches to reaffirm their commitment to the quest of the visible unity of the church in a new and meaningful way. It is of utmost importance that they overcome their differences, move beyond the present crisis, and walk in repentance and humility towards Christ's last and most significant will "that they may all be one" (John 17:21).

No doubt the member churches are deeply divided about where the emphasis should be placed in their quest for the visible unity of the church: on the sacramental act of eucharist, which the traditional churches, and especially the Orthodox, consider as the sine qua non of all efforts; or on the church's socio-cosmic responsibility and on the "unity of humankind" (along with the "unity of the church")? The former is clearly determined by the term "eucharistic vision", which has dominated the ecumenical field ever since the Vancouver assembly (1983); the latter has been on the agenda of all ecumenical projects since the Uppsala assembly (1968) and is expressed by such phrases as "costly unity" and "costly commitment" of recent WCC projects. Unless a common understanding between the Orthodox (as well as the Roman Catholic) and the Protestant member churches on this issue is achieved, no real progress on the ecumenical movement, at least within the WCC as its institutional expression, can take place.

This book is an attempt to tackle this most dividing issue, which lies at the heart of the present crisis of the ecumenical movement, as far as the WCC priorities are concerned. It consists of 11 previously prepared studies, all of which were undertaken during the last ten years on various ecumenical occasions. All of them focus in one way or another on the eucharistic understanding of the church's identity, which is the normative Orthodox approach to ecclesiology.

The target readership of the book is both the mainstream constituency of the ecumenical movement, which shows an understandable scepticism towards the significance of the eucharist for the advance of ecumenism, and the Orthodox constituency, which has never ceased to complain about the overemphasis in the WCC on social issues. I intend to move beyond the old scholastic, sacramentalistic view of the eucharist and to rediscover the diaconal dimension of this sacrament par excellence of the church, which is in fact the authentic biblical and patristic view.

I belong to the new generation of Orthodox theologians, who, like our great predecessors, are fervent about the ecumenical imperative. Unlike most of the Orthodox who are seriously engaged in the ecumenical dialogue, I do not feel obliged to defend our traditional viewpoint. Rather, I envisage a common understanding of our common witness, one that both respects the church's great tradition and takes into account current ecumenical concerns.

1. Towards a Costly Eucharistic Vision: A Jubilee Bible Study on John 13:1-20

With the following words, an Orthodox hymn composed almost a thousand years ago for the matins of holy Thursday, the traditional day of commemoration of the institution by our Lord of the mystery of the eucharist, stresses the close connection between eucharist and diakonia.

> Interpreting, O Lord, the mystery of the eucharist (*mystagōgōn*)
> to your disciples, you were teaching them saying:
> Behold, my friends, no fear should separate you from me;
> for though I suffer, I do so for the life of the world.
> Be not scandalized in me, for I came not to be served
> but to serve and give my life a ransom for the sake of the world.
> If, therefore, you wish to consider yourselves my friends,
> you must imitate me.
> Whoever wants to be first, let that one be last;
> whoever wants to be master, let that one behave like a servant.
> Remain in communion with me, in order to bear the true wine,
> for I am the vine of life.

With the approach of Harare 1998, the assembly marking the jubilee of the WCC, member churches more than ever need to reaffirm the goal of the visible unity of the church. One element of deep concern, perhaps not admitted so openly, is a basic division among member churches over what the church should emphasize: the sacramental act of eucharist, or the church's socio-cosmic responsibilities. Traditional churches view the former as the sine qua non of all efforts, which is reflected in the emphasis on "eucharist vision", noted since the Vancouver assembly (1983). Since the Uppsala assembly (1968), however, the latter has been prominent in all ecumenical projects, reflected in the ideas of "costly unity" and "costly commitment".

John 13:1-20, which has been chosen as one of the biblical pericopes for reflection by the churches on their way to the coming jubilee assembly, is a perfect example of how inter-related sacrament and service, eucharist and diakonia, actually are, thus making the above dilemma a pseudo-dilemma.

Diakonia – the act of serving God and ministering to him not only in the conventional cultic way but mainly and primarily to his entire creation (humanity, created in his own image in order to achieve his likeness [Gen. 1:26-27; 5:1; 9:6 etc.], as well as the whole cosmos, i.e. entire created world [Gen. 1:1ff.]) – is the ultimate expression of Christian faith in the midst of the tremendous sufferings in the world and within each local Christian community. The profound meaning of diakonia is nowhere better expressed in Christian life and theology than in the eucharist.

The understanding of this mystery par excellence of church, not as a mere cultic rite, but as the radical expression of the church's identity as a proleptic manifestation in this world of the kingdom of God, a dynamic act of communion, love, sacrifice and sharing, is wonderfully presented by the author of the fourth gospel, our first theologian who most powerfully commented on the eucharist.

Jesus' Washing the Disciples' Feet (John 13:1-20): A Diaconal Understanding of Eucharist

Though he omits from his gospel the words of institutions of the eucharist, on which unfortunately for so many years all scholarly approaches to the eucharist were exclusively centred, St John the Evangelist is rightly considered the "sacramental" theologian of the New Testament. The ecclesiological symbolism of the vine and the branches in the "farewell discourse" (ch. 15), the flow of blood and water from the pierced side of the crucified Jesus (19:34), the miraculous change of water into wine at the wedding in Cana at the outset of Jesus' earthly ministry (2:1-11), chapter 6 with its "eucharistic discourse" (especially vv.51b-58), the mysterious reference in 3:5 to the necessity of the believer's rebirth "of *water* and Spirit", and above all the washing of the disciples' feet by Jesus himself (ch. 13) all make the "sacramental", or rather "eucharistic", character of the fourth gospel more than inescapable. The issue at stake here, however, is the proper understanding of eucharist by the fourth evangelist.

1. To recover the overall Johannine eucharistic theology, one undoubtedly must turn to chapter 6. There we have the beginnings of what has become axiomatic in later Christian tradition: to have "eternal life" (i.e. to live an authentic and not just a conventional life) one must

be in communion with Christ. Communion with Christ, however, means participation in the perfect communion that exists within the Holy Trinity between the Father and the Son ("Just as the living Father sent me, and I live because of the Father, so whoever eats me will live because of me", 6:57). What we have here in John is in fact a parallel expression to what became in later patristic literature the biblical foundation of the doctrine of *theosis* (divinization; cf. the classic statement of 2 Pet. 1:4, "participants of the divine nature"). In the case of the gospel of John, however, this idea is expressed in a less abstract way.

Taking this argument a little further, one can say that John developed more fully the interpretation of the eucharist as the unceasingly repeated act of sealing the "new covenant" of God with his new people. This interpretation is evidenced also in the earlier synoptic and Pauline tradition, although there the covenantal interpretation of Jesus' death in the phrase "this is my blood of the *covenant*" (Mark 14:24 par. and 1 Cor. 11:25) is somewhat hidden by the soteriological formula "that is poured out *for* you/many" (Luke 22:20).

This eucharist theology of John, with the direct emphasis on the idea of the covenant and of communion, is in fact in accordance with Jeremiah's vision, which was at the same time also a promise. The only difference is that in John these ideas have become a central feature. Just as in the book of the prophet Jeremiah, so also in John, the ideas of a new covenant, of communion, and of the church as a people are most strongly emphasized. Listen to what the prophet was saying: "I will make a new *covenant*" (Jer. 31:31) and "I will give them a heart to know that I am the Lord; and they shall be my *people*" (Jer. 24:7).

2. The covenantal dimension of eucharist, however, is not the only feature emphasized in the gospel of John. The pericope of the washing of the disciples' feet (13:1-20) reveals a further aspect of the understanding of eucharist by the fourth evangelist. The incident in question, which is preserved only by St John, is placed in the context of the last supper and in direct connection with Judas's betrayal; in other words, exactly in the place the synoptic gospels have recorded the so-called dominical sayings of the institution of the eucharist (Mark 14:22-25 par.). Since it is virtually certain that John knew of the synoptic tradition, one can fairly argue that he has actually replaced the account of the institution of the eucharist by the symbolic act of Jesus' washing his disciples' feet. A careful reading of the reference to the new commandment of love (13:34-35), in the same context, brings immediately to mind the institution narrative. The "*new* commandment" sounds very similar to

the "*new* covenant" of the so-called institution narratives of the synoptic tradition. If the eucharist is the most precious legacy Jesus has left to the world, then one should approach this legacy in the way he himself interpreted it, at least according to the fourth evangelist, i.e. as an act of diakonia, humility and sharing. In his society the washing of a disciple's feet was more than an ultimate act of humble and kenotic diakonia; it was an act of radical social behaviour, in fact a rite of inversion of roles within the society. Moreover, the Lord himself has commanded his disciples, and through them his church: "I have set you an example, that *you also should do as I have done to you*" (John 13:15). In all gospel traditions Jesus is presented in the way he himself described his mission, namely as the one who came down to this world "not to be served but to serve" (Mark 10:45 par.).

In sum, it is fair to argue that the gospel of John understands the eucharist not as a mere cultic and sacramental act, but primarily as a diaconal act and an alternative way of life with clear social implications. This understanding is already evidenced in Luke, though not in such an explicit form as in John (cf. Luke 22:24-27).

3. According to modern theological scholarship (biblical and liturgical), the eucharist was "lived" in the early Christian community as a foretaste of the coming kingdom of God, a proleptic manifestation within the tragic realities of history of an authentic life of communion, unity, justice and equality, with no practical differentiation (soteriological or otherwise) between men and women. This is, after all, the real meaning of what St John has called "eternal life". And because of this eucharistic experience, according to some historians, the church came up with the doctrine of Trinity, the grandest expression ever produced in theology.

If this was the authentic, original meaning of the eucharist, then the redaction by the author of the fourth gospel of another pericope full of ritual connotation and closely related to the "eucharistic" incident of the washing of the disciples' feet – namely that of the anointing of Jesus (John 12:1-8) – may not be accidental. The evangelist not only placed this famous pericope in the same Passover setting as the pericope of the washing of the disciples' feet (John 13:1-20), he also replaced the unknown woman by Mary, a figure from within Lazarus's family, which Jesus greatly loved. The point for discussion here is that by actually replacing the original, and certainly more authentic, place of the pouring of the "very costly ointment of nard" from Jesus' hair (Mark 14:3; Matt. 26:7, originally understood as a prophetic act of messianic character, parallel to St Peter's confession at Caesarea of Philippi, Mark 8:27-30 par.) to Jesus' feet (John 12:3), John made a woman anticipate the incident of Jesus himself washing his disciples' feet. By so doing, the "disciple of love" (according to the Christian tradition) changed even an act of witness into an act of diakonia.

4. If any conclusion is to be drawn from the Johannine eucharistic understanding, it is to affirm the ecclesial and diaconal dimension of the eucharist as a communion event and not as an act of personal devotion; an act of diakonia and sharing, and not a sacramentalistic, quasi-marginal rite; an expression of the church as the people *(laos)* and household *(oikos)* of God and as the body of Christ mystically united with its head and a proleptic manifestation of the kingdom to come, and not a mere cultic or witnessing institution. In other words, the eucharist as the unique and primary sacrament of the church is a reflection of the communion that exists between the persons of the Holy Trinity. In such a situation one can "fulfil the law of Christ" only by carrying "one another's burdens" (Gal. 6:2).

A Historical and Theological Reflection

The importance of the eucharist and of "eucharistic theology" (more precisely of "eucharistic ecclesiology") in the ecumenical debate has only recently been rediscovered and realized. The issue at stake, however, is whether the eucharistic vision, for which the WCC speaks, is at all related to a sacramentalistic view of the eucharist, of the mystery par excellence of the one undivided, holy, catholic, and apostolic church.

The proper understanding of the eucharist has been always a stumbling-block in Christian theology and life – not only at the start of the Christian community, when the church had to struggle against a multitude of mystery cults, but also much later, even within the ecumenical era. In vain have distinguished theologians of the East (most notably in the case of Cabasilas) attempted to redefine Christian sacramental theology on the basis of trinitarian theology. Seen from a modern theological perspective, this was a desperate attempt to reject certain tendencies that overemphasized the importance of Christology at the expense of the role of the Holy Spirit. The theological issues of filioque and the epiclesis have been thoroughly discussed, and great progress has been achieved in recent years through initiatives undertaken jointly by the WCC and the Roman Catholic Church, but their real consequences for the meaning of the sacramental theology of the church have yet to be fully and systematically examined. After all, one should not forget that one of the main focuses during the Reformation (rightly so!) was the sacramentalistic understanding of the eucharist, which has resulted in the dialectic opposition between sacramentalism and the complete rejection of sacraments. To some historians this was the main reason for the tragic secularization of our society and the transformation of the church into a religion – in some cases a cultic religion, and in other cases merely one that proclaims or confesses.

Furthermore, the whole ecclesiological process – from the eschatological kerygma of Jesus of Nazareth, announcing the coming of the kingdom of God in his mission, to the understanding by the first apostles of their mission to evangelize the world as a sign of the eschaton, and further down to the Ignatian concept of the church as a eucharistic community – clearly reveals a stress on the *eschatological* nature of the church, not its nature as hierarchical (and therefore authoritative), sacramentalistic, or even simply proclaiming. The early Christian community understood itself as portraying the kingdom of God on earth, the restoration of the "household" of God, in its majestic eschatological splendour; and the primary concern of the great theologians of the apostolic and post-apostolic period was exactly to maintain clearly that vision and also reality before the eyes of the faithful. This is the meaning of the centrality of eucharist and of the ministries related to it.

Again "trinitarian theology" best elucidates the eucharist, which not only is the mystery of church but also is a projection of the inner dynamics (love, communion, equality, diaconia, sharing etc.) of the Holy Trinity into the world and cosmic realities. The ecclesiological problem for our churches, which is of such vital importance for the ecumenical movement, is thus a matter not so much of doctrinal accommodation or of organization and structure (faith and order) but of a diaconal attitude and an eschatological orientation. It truly involves a *costly eucharistic vision*.

2. Orthodoxy and Ecumenism

The Orthodox church, which in the past has played an important role in the ecumenical endeavour through the initiative of the Ecumenical Patriarchate, and whose participation in the WCC, the main forum of the multilateral ecumenical dialogue, is so vital, is faced today with a number of problems. On the one hand, there is a growing dissatisfaction with the results of the ecumenical dialogue so far and a dangerous shift towards Orthodox "fundamentalism", especially in countries of Eastern Europe, but also in the Middle East (cf. the case of the Orthodox Patriarchate of Jerusalem). Within some Orthodox circles some are seriously considering, or pressing in the direction of, abandoning any ecumenical effort, even withdrawing from all multilateral and bilateral forums of ecumenical dialogue. On the other hand, recent promising events have made clear the authentic ecumenical character of Orthodoxy and reaffirmed its commitment to the search for the visible unity of the church and its struggle for the unity of humankind, more precisely of the entire created world. Such events include the strong leadership of His All-Holiness the Ecumenical Patriarch Mgr Bartholomeos, who with his initiatives and speeches is directing Orthodoxy towards an authentic ecumenism;[1] the recent decision of the holy synod of the Moscow Patriarchate to reject the motion to withdraw from the ecumenical dialogue, despite strong pressure from the anti-ecumenists;[2] the successful and pleasant outcome of the official theological dialogue of the Orthodox church with the family of the Oriental Orthodox churches (the so-called non-Chalcedonian churches, which broke communion with the still-undivided, one, catholic church in the fifth century but, despite their separation, maintained the same teaching as mainstream Eastern Orthodoxy, even in Christology);[3] and finally the establishment in 1993 of the Society of Ecumenical Studies and Inter-Orthodox Relations, based and legally functioning in Thessaloniki,[4] as well as the recent decision of the University of Thessaloniki to set up an ecumenical institute.

● An earlier version of this chapter appeared in *Oikoumene and Theology: The 1993-95 Erasmus Lectures in Ecumenical Theology*, EKO 11, Thessaloniki, 1996, pp.145-82, and is reprinted here by permission of the publisher.

In order correctly to assess Orthodoxy's attitude towards ecumenism and fully and profoundly appreciate its role in today's ecumenical dialogue, it is absolutely necessary to examine the two stages of its ecumenical encounter: (1) with the West; and (2) with contextual theologies. To do so, we need first to examine the theological presuppositions of this encounter, which will become clear once we define the identity of Orthodoxy.

Defining the Identity of Orthodoxy

Whenever the Orthodox have to speak about "Orthodoxy", they find themselves in a very strange and difficult situation. What can they say about the specifics of "Orthodoxy" at a time when the adjective "orthodox" itself is widely understood as having more or less negative connotations? In Western theological circles Orthodox theology has become known through the ecumenical discussions, especially within the WCC. Some people identify Orthodoxy with a kind of Roman Catholicism without a pope or with a kind of Protestantism with episcopacy. To most Protestants (certainly those from the "evangelical" stream of the Christian tradition, but sometimes also those from the "ecumenical") *Orthodoxia* (Orthodoxy) has come to signify stagnation in church life, strict dogmatic confessionalism, inflexibility and unreadiness to adapt to modern situations – at best an "Eastern phenomenon" vis-à-vis the "Western mentality" and perhaps "Western theological process". Almost a generation ago S. McCrae Cavert, a pioneer in the ecumenical movement, gave this introduction to his own high appreciation of the Orthodox tradition:

> My textbooks in church history made little or no reference to Eastern Orthodoxy after the Great Schism between East and West in 1054 – or at least after the fall of Constantinople in 1453. I assumed that the Orthodox church was static and impervious to renewal, weighted down under the dead hand of the past. I thought of it as preoccupied with an endless repetition of ancient rituals unrelated to the ongoing currents of life in today's world. The practice of involving all the saints and reverencing icons appeared to me as expressions of unenlightened credulity. The ascetic and monastic forms of life looked like outmoded medievalism. The long centuries of subservience of church to the state struck me as intolerable. A sacramental mysticism seemed to me to have taken the place of prophetic mission in contemporary society.[5]

Quite recently D. J. Bosch, in his book *Transforming Mission: Paradigm Shifts in Theology of Mission*, concludes his chapter on the mission paradigm of the Eastern church with a similar assessment:

The church adapted to the existing world order, resulting in Church and Society penetrating and permeating each other. The role of religion – any religion – in society is that of both stabilizer and emancipator; it is both mythical and messianic. In the Eastern tradition the church tended to express the former of each of these pairs rather than the latter. The emphasis was on conservation and restoration, rather than on embarking on a journey into the unknown. The key words were "tradition", "orthodoxy", and the "fathers", and the church became the bulwark of right doctrine. Orthodox churches tended to become ingrown, excessively nationalistic, and without a concern for those outside.

In particular, Platonic categories of thought all but destroyed primitive Christian eschatology. The church established itself in the world as an institute of almost exclusively other-worldly salvation.[6]

This assessment of Orthodoxy was actually reinforced by the first Orthodox, mostly immigrants from old Russia, who came in contact with the West after a long period of separation, and who in their desperate attempt to preserve their Orthodox identity in a world that was quite alien to them and to present it to their fellow Christians in the West emphasized the mystical aspect of the Orthodox theology. This is notably the case with V. Lossky, who in his monumental work *The Mystical Theology of the Eastern Church* has virtually determined the character of Orthodoxy in the ecumenical scene.[7] Today this one-sided, mystical presentation of Orthodoxy is challenged by various voices, one being Ion Bria, who rejoices in the existence of a variety of trends – sometimes even contradictory – within modern Orthodox theology.[8] We therefore need radically to redefine the above understanding of the term, which is totally misleading with regard to the identity of the Eastern Orthodox church. *Orthodoxia*, according to most serious interpreters of its tradition, means the wholeness of the people of God who share the *orthē doxa* (right conviction/opinion) concerning the event of God's salvation in Christ and his church, as well as the *orthopraxia* (right expression) of this faith. *Orthodoxia* leads to the maximum possible application in *orthopraxia* of charismatic life in the freedom of the Holy Spirit in all aspects of daily life in society and the cosmos. Everybody is invited by Orthodoxy to transcend confessions and inflexible institutions without necessarily denying them. N. Nissiotis has reminded us that Orthodoxy is not to be identified only with us who are Orthodox in the historical sense, with all our limitations and shortcomings. "We should never forget that this term is given to the one (holy, catholic and) apostolic church as a whole over against the heretics who, of their own choice, split from the main body of the church. The term is exclusive for all those who willingly fall away from the historical stream of life of the one church, but it is inclusive for those who profess their spiritual belonging to that stream."[9]

The question is, How can one profess his or her "orthodoxy"? How can he or she establish it? On what ground and from what sources? The Roman Catholics have Vatican II to draw from; the Orthodox do not. The Lutherans have an Augsburg Confession of their own; the Orthodox do not, and they also lack the equivalent of a Luther or a Calvin to give them their theological identity. The only authoritative sources they possess are in fact common to the rest of the Christians: the Bible and the tradition. How can one establish a distinctly Orthodox view on a basis that is common to non-Orthodox as well?

Some Orthodox insist that Othodox theology is not a matter of drawing from special sources but of interpreting the sources the Orthodox share with the rest of the Christians.[10] In other words, it is a matter of theological presuppositions, which suggests a certain problematic and method not always familiar to the non-Orthodox. Naturally, then, all their theological viewpoints come only as the logical consequence of these presuppositions.

Orthodoxy and the West: The Main Theological Characteristics of Orthodoxy

The essence of Orthodoxy, vis-a-vis Western theology in its entirety, both Catholic and Protestant, is beyond theological presuppositions per se. I would dare say it is *a way of life*, hence the importance of its liturgical tradition. Of course theological presuppositions and liturgical experience are very closely connected with each other. It is exactly for this reason that the Orthodox have placed the liturgy in such a prominent place in their theology. In fact, it is widely held that the liturgical dimension is perhaps the only safe criterion for ascertaining the unique thrust of Orthodox theology. The church is first of all a worshiping community. Worship comes first, doctrine and discipline second. The *lex orandi* has a privileged priority in the life of the Christian church. The *lex credendi* depends on the devotional experience and vision of the church, as G. Florovsky put it,[11] or more precisely on the authentic (i.e. liturgical) identity of the church.[12] The heart of Orthodox liturgy, as in all or almost all Christian traditions, is the eucharist, which the Orthodox call divine liturgy. The criterion most widely held among Orthodox of our time for determining Orthodox theology is undoubtedly the eucharistic approach to all aspects of theology,[13] and especially to ecclesiology. It is only in the eucharist that the church becomes church in its fullest sense.

Eucharist is conceived of as the very manifestation of the church and as a corporate act of the whole community. Orthodox theology has been known to non-Orthodox as the more consistent with eucharistic ecclesiology, while Roman catholic theology puts more emphasis on universal ecclesiology.[14]

Closely connected to, in fact as a consequence of, the liturgical-eucharistic criterion, which constitutes for the Orthodox the only living *depositum fidei*, Orthodox theology is also determined by the following criteria: (1) the idea of the living tradition, (2) the trinitarian basis for all theology, (3) the pneumatological dimension, (4) the eschatological perspective and (5) the cosmic dimension of its identity.[15]

Tradition. Orthodox reverence for tradition arises from a sense of living continuity with the church of the ancient, apostolic period. Behind it lies the same determination that kept the unity of the two Testaments against the attempt by the Gnostic Marcion to reject the Old Testament. The Orthodox do not consider tradition as something in addition to, or over against, the Bible. Scripture and tradition are not treated as two different things, two distinct sources of the Christian faith. Scripture exists within tradition, which, although it gives a unique pre-eminence to the Bible, also includes further developments of the apostolic faith – in the form of clarification and explication, not of addition.[16] It is even more important that the Orthodox conception of Tradition, as distinguished from the various local or regional or even temporal traditions, is not a static entity but a dynamic reality, not a dead acceptance of the past but a living experience of the Holy Spirit in the present.[17] In G. Florovsky's words, "Tradition is the witness of the Spirit; the Spirit's unceasing revelation and preaching of the Good News.... It is not only a protective, conservative principle, but primarily the principle of growth and renewal."[18]

The trinitarian basis. All fundamental aspects of Orthodox theology – creation of the entire cosmos by God, redemption in Christ and salvation through the church but, beyond its boundaries, in the power of the Holy Spirit etc. – are conceived as the natural consequence of the inner dynamics of the triune God. All originate from the communion and love that exist within the Holy Trinity.

Applied to *mission*, this trinitarian basis has had the tremendous effect of helping the church to avoid imperialistic or confessionalistic attitudes.[19] "The trinitarian theology points to the fact that God's involvement in history aims at drawing humanity and creation in general into this communion with God's very life. The implications of this assertion for understanding mission are very important: mission does not aim primarily at the propagation or transmission of intellectual convictions, doctrines, moral commands etc., but at the transmission of the life of communion that exists in God."[20]

Of similar importance is the application of trinitarian theology to the *structure of the church*, at least in theory. By nature, the church cannot reflect the worldly image of a secular organization, which is based on power and domination. Rather, it embraces the kenotic image of the Holy Trinity, which is based on love and communion.[21] If we take a little further this trinitarian understanding of ecclesiology, taking into consideration the distinction of the hypostases (persons) within the Holy Trinity, we realize that the church is a church of "God" (the Father) before it becomes a church of "Christ" and of a certain place. That is why in the Orthodox liturgy all the proper eucharistic prayers are addressed to God. This theology has revealing implications on a number of issues, ranging from the profound meaning of episcopacy (with the bishop as image of "Christ") to the dialectics between Christ and church, divine and human, as well as the unity of man and woman.

Pneumatology. Much has been written and said about Orthodox spirituality. But very often this spirituality is understood in the Western sense, as an idealistic philosophical category, as a way of life distinct from, or in opposition to, the material life – as if it referred to the spirit of human beings and not to the Spirit of God, which in the biblical sense (2 Cor. 13:13) is by definition conditioned by the idea of *koinonia* (communion). Here we may again note the eucharistic dimension of the church as the gathering of the people of God *epi to auto* (at the same [place], i.e. together; cf. Acts 2:1, 44 etc.) and as the "communion of the saints". The Spirit is incompatible with individualism, its primary work being the transformation of all reality to a relational status.[22]

Western theology in the past has very often been criticized for being "christomonistic", of orienting almost all its attention to Christ, relegating the Spirit to an ancillary role (variously as agent of Christ, inspirer of the prophets and the authors of the Bible, helper of the church to listen, apprehend and interpret the word of God etc.). This criticism may have gone too far and may be an exaggeration.[23] It shows, however, the implicit pneumatological orientation of the Orthodox tradition. This orientation, however, has never taken the form of a "pneumatomonism". Rather, it has led to an understanding of Christology conditioned in a constitutive way by pneumatology. The most important distinctives of Orthodox pneumatology are (1) the rejection of the filioque theology; (2)

the importance of the epiclesis, i.e. the invocation of the Holy Spirit in all liturgical practices, especially in the eucharistic anaphora; and (3) the understanding of all the church's ministries always within the context of the community.

Starting with the third distinctive, I can only stress the fact that the Orthodox church has not till recently had to cope with clericalism and anti-clericalism, or tension between clergy and laity. To me, this explains why the thorny question of the ordination of women has not come up as an issue and a serious challenge from within the Orthodox church.

With regard to epiclesis, I will simply mention that the daily liturgical cycle of the Orthodox church is introduced by the following well-known prayer to the Holy Spirit:

> O heavenly King, Comforter, the Spirit of truth, present in all places and filling all things, treasury of good things and giver of life, come dwell among us, purify us from every stain, and of your goodness save our souls.[24]

It is therefore significant that in the Orthodox liturgy and in particular in all sacraments (called by the Orthodox "mysteries", not "sacraments" in the conventional sense), it is the Spirit who is repeatedly invoked. Furthermore, the sacrament of chrismation (the equivalent of the Western confirmation), which is always understood as the seal of the gift of the Holy Spirit, has never been dissociated from baptism. Above all, in the Orthodox church it has always been believed that the transformation (note here the neutral *metabolē*, not the scholastic *transubstantiatio*) of the holy gifts takes place during the invocation of the Holy Spirit, not during the utterance of the dominical words of the institution of the eucharist. In addition, the epiclesis of the Holy Spirit in Eastern Orthodox liturgy is made for both the holy gifts and the community (in fact first for the community and then for the holy gifts). The Orthodox claim that the church, in its fullest sense, is nowhere manifested but in the eucharist as a communion-event is therefore well justified. The church is not only an institution, i.e. something which is given; it is above all a communion-event. We may say that Christ institutes the church, but it is the Holy Spirit who constitutes it.[25]

Finally, with regard to the filioque issue, it has been implicitly acknowledged, even by Roman Catholics (cf. e. g. Y. Congar), that with this unnecessary insertion into the Nicene Creed, "the charism is made subordinate to the institution, inner freedom to imposed authority, prophetism to juridicism, mysticism to scholasticism, the laity to the clergy, the universal priesthood to the ministerial hierarchy, and finally the college of bishops to the primacy of the Pope."[26] Without considering the filioque as an error on the part of Western theology,[27] its rejection in the East is a clear indication of the Orthodox church's consciousness of the need to safeguard the role and the significance of the Holy Spirit in the life of the church. By rejecting any idea of subordination of the Holy Spirit within the economy of the Holy Trinity, the Orthodox have kept alive the idea of renewal and the concept of the church as a continuous Pentecost.

The church as an eschatological reality. The ecclesiological problem, which is so important an issue in today's ecumenical discussions, is a matter not so much of church organization and structure as of eschatological orientation (cf. ch. 8 below). The whole Christian tradition – from Jesus' preaching the coming of the kingdom of God (the already inaugurated, but not yet fulfilled, new heaven and new earth), through the Ignatian concept of the church as a eucharistic community (with the bishop as the image of Christ), and down to the later Orthodox tradition (which, by the way, understands the eucharist as the mystery of the church and not merely as one mystery among others) – reveals that the eschatological, not the hierarchical (episcopal, conciliar, congregational etc.), nature of the church has been stressed.[28] In Orthodox theology and liturgical praxis the church does not draw its identity from what it is or from what was given to it as an institution but from what it will be, i.e. from the eschaton. According to Orthodox theology, the church is understood as portraying the kingdom of God on earth, in fact as being a glimpse or foretaste of the kingdom to come. This is the inevitable consequence of the main concern of all great theologians (of the apostolic, post-apostolic and later periods of the Orthodox church) to maintain clearly the vision of that kingdom before the eyes of the people. Hence the episcopocentric structure of the church as an essential part of that vision. The bishop as presiding in love in the eucharist is not a vicar or representative or ambassador of Christ but an *eikōn* (image) of Christ. So with the rest of the ministries of the church: they are not parallel to, or given by, Christ but rather are identical with those of Christ.[29]

For the same reason, the whole of Orthodox theology and life is centred on the resurrection. The church exists not because Christ died on the cross but because he is risen from the dead, thus becoming the *aparchē* (first-fruits) of all humanity. Eschatology, contrary to its usual treatment as the last chapter of dogmatics in almost all Western theological handbooks, constitutes the primary aspect, the beginning of the church, that which gives it its identity, sustains and inspires its very existence. Hence the kingdom of God is primary in all ecclesiological considerations. In the Orthodox church everything belongs to the kingdom. The church does not administer all reality; it only prepares the way for the kingdom. That is why, although to the eyes of the historian and the sociologist the church is yet another human community or society, to the Orthodox it is primarily a mystery.[30] The Orthodox often call it an icon of the kingdom to come.

The cosmic dimension of Orthodox theology. The Orthodox conception of the church is not that of a communion of human beings unrelated to creation. In ecumenical circles the contribution of the Orthodox theology is well known for its so-called holistic approach to salvation, a balance between the horizontal and vertical, between the human and the cosmic dimensions. Here, I would like to emphasize the significance of the mysteries/sacraments, and especially of the eucharist, which are considered so crucial to the Orthodox, even more crucial than the preaching of the word.[31] In the eucharist humanity acts as the priest of creation, referring it (anaphora) to God and allowing it to become part of the body of Christ and thus to survive eternally.[32]

* * *

These are only some of the basic aspects of the Eastern Orthodox tradition vis-à-vis the Western tradition. Sometimes I have deliberately overemphasized the differences between them, but only to make them clearer, for I firmly believe in a synthesis of the two.[33] The authentic catholicity of the church must include both East and West. To recall just one area of the above analysis, Western theology tends to limit ecclesiology to the historical context. The church ends up being completely historicized, and thus it ceases to be the manifestation of the eschaton, becoming instead an image of this world. At the other end, Eastern theology, with its vision of future or heavenly things, runs the danger of disincarnating the church from history. A dynamic encounter will enrich both traditions. Orthodoxy, however, has not come to terms and dialogued only with the West. More recently it has encountered also the South, from which the newest and most dynamic part of Christianity has sprung. And if with Western theology there was a common point of reference in a theology "from above", with the South the theological encounter must take place on a different level, in terms of a theology "from below".

Orthodoxy and Contextual Theologies

The seventh assembly of the WCC in Canberra (February 1991) dramatically illustrated the problems with this kind of ecumenical dialogue.[34] This happened in spite of recommendations from the previous assembly (Vancouver 1983) to develop a "vital, coherent theology" capable of creatively blending classical theology with contextual theology, the theoretical with the practical, the continuing (tradition) with the relative (current problems and issues).

A problem of methodology. In the Canberra assembly two antithetical theologies came into conflict, two different approaches were taken towards the assembly's main theme (the Holy Spirit).[35] The confrontation came to light not so much in the two diametrically opposite main presentations at the assembly – the "orthodox", "classical", theological, "academic" presentation by Mgr Parthenios, the Orthodox patriarch of Alexandria; and the "sound and light", "contextual", non-traditional presentation by the South Korean Presbyterian professor Chung Hyun-Kyung – as in the reaction that followed, above all from the Orthodox.[36] The Orthodox gave the impression – not entirely correctly – that Orthodox theology and contextual theology are in conflict.[37] Those familiar with the issue know that the debate concerns methodology, and only coincidentally was it related to Orthodoxy as such. Even the joint Canberra-Chambésy statement by the Orthodox,[38] though it has had a positive effect on redefining the WCC's priorities, did not touch upon, or even marginally refer to, the problem of theological methodology.

Within ecumenical circles it is certainly well known that in the area of multilateral dialogues, even after many disappointing attempts, it has been impossible to achieve any sustained momentum for a unified and commonly acceptable theology, a common language of communication. There does not exist a single, unifying "ecumenical theology", although this has less to do with content than with methodology.[39] Fr Ion Bria very rightly emphasizes that differences in theological methodology play an important role in contemporary ecumenical debate. He comes to the candid conclusion that "the basic framework in which many ecumenical subjects are discussed is not home to the Eastern churches.... We need more clarity in defining the unity of tradition since many aspects of Orthodox rhetoric concerning the unity of the church can easily be misunderstood."[40]

We do not pretend in this study to answer the question concerning the relation between Orthodox theology and contextual theologies, nor the place of contextual theology in ecumenical dialogue. Rather, I simply attempt to open the subject, since I believe that the future creative contribution and substantive participation of the Orthodox church in, and the contribution of the Orthodox theology to, the ecumenical dialogue and the WCC depend very much on recognizing, understanding and finding a dynamic solution to this burning methodological issue.[41]

Contextual theology is itself closely linked with the problem of theological methodology. And theological methodology – how to "do theology", how to work out the use of theology as a tool for unity – is something that has seriously engaged the WCC for some time, and especially the Faith and Order unit, which has been enlarged with the formal participation of the Roman Catholic Church in the WCC. Indeed, during the triennium 1972-74 the Ecumenical Institute in Bossey hosted a series of three conferences on the general theme "Dogmatic or Contextual Theology".[42]

A sketch of the ecumenical methodologies. In order better to understand the current methodological problematic, it is necessary briefly to review the history of theological methodology in ecumenical dialogue and to point out the successive trends that have dominated the WCC and Faith and Order, since these methodologies continue to be used[43] in the process of the churches' search for visible unity.

Of extreme importance for our present subject, especially concerning the creative and constructive relations between Orthodox theology and the non-Orthodox Christian world of the WCC, is the 1971 Louvain conference of the Faith and Order commission. That occasion marks the first use of contextual terminology in a formal statement of the ecumenical dialogue, as it mentioned "intercontextual method" and "intercontextual approach".[44] After this point, the Orthodox generally began to take a more guarded and even critical attitude towards the various programmes of the WCC, while at the same time this foremost ecumenical body clearly turned in the direction of the wider community and other issues of humanity.[45]

This schematic differentiation between two periods of Orthodox participation in the ecumenical movement as a whole, and similarly within the WCC,[46] has been noted also by a number of important Orthodox theologians involved in the ecumenical movement. According to Fr Ion Bria, the first period, typified by the Toronto statement (1950), entitled "The Church, the Churches and the World Council of Churches",[47] was the stage of introductions, of coming to know others. During the second period, however, interest shifted from theory to practice, from theology to anthropology, and emphasis was unquestionably on social Christian witness.[48] The clear awareness of responsibility for correcting the historical divisions, the scandal of schism and the fragmentation of the oneness of the body of Christ, now gave place to interest as well in showing solidarity with those (the laos) engaged in the struggle for justice, peace and liberation. The uneasiness of the Orthodox – which became increasingly conspicuous even towards the end of the first period – towards the explicit dualism that was dominating the ecumenical movement (horizontal-vertical dimension of salvation, visible-invisible church, institutional-empirical etc.) was now transformed into complete opposition. Indeed, 1973 marked a point of almost open break with the WCC, when two autocephalous Orthodox churches questioned in the most unequivocal way the direction being taken by the WCC, beginning with the division placed between the horizontal and vertical dimensions of salvation and the relation of dogmatic theology to contextual theology.[49] At this point we must remind ourselves that at that critical moment, when the very presence of the Orthodox in the WCC and the ecumenical movement was at risk,[50] it was judged necessary to convene an ad hoc Orthodox consulatation at New Valaamo, Finland (1977). There, with the backing of historical and theological evidence, the ecumenical character and orientation of the church and Orthodoxy was once again confirmed.[51]

But how did the WCC ever since the 1970s gradually come to adopt almost exclusively the method of contextual theology in its discussions and, more important, in its policy-making? Here we must remember that all the preceding methodologies that were used as tools for dialogue in the first stage of the ecumenical movement were proven to be ineffective in sustaining the initial optimism for overcoming the divisions of the Christian world. Both the *comparative method*, necessary and extremely constructive for the initial stage of the dialogue,[52] and its later descendant the *dialectical method*, which made its appearance at the first assembly of the WCC (Amsterdam 1948) after a proposal by Karl Barth,[53] led the ecumenical dialogue to a dead end, since the various sides quite naturally remained firmly entrenched. Furthermore, this methodology effectively enclosed ecumenical dialogue within the dialectical antithesis of "Catholic-Protestant", with the result that the Orthodox had to struggle tremendously to point out and clarify the distinctly different texture of authentic Orthodox spirituality and theology.[54]

The next phase in the ecumenical dialogue began with the introduction of the *christological method* at the third international Faith and Order conference in Lund (1952).[55] This had an Archimedean effect, and once again the ecumenical world was set in motion. Using "the Christ-event" as the point of departure, the churches – the essential partners in the dialogue – agreed to abandon the comparative and dialectical approaches and the various presuppositions attached to them, and instead "to show the points of agreement that form the basis for the gift of unity [in Christ] and to apply this to the entire range of divisions until such time that the very last pocket of dispute that prevents confessional unity is erased".[56]

But this method, in spite of the invaluable help it gave in approaching basic issues, and especially in the drafting of theological studies and the formulation of ecclesiological positions for progress towards visible unity,[57] also quickly proved to be inadequate.[58] Its main weakness could be traced to an overemphasis on christocentricity. Theologically, this subordinated the trinitarian and pneumatological foundations of Christian faith,[59] and it led as well to an overemphasis on eschatology. Besides minimizing these substantial differences, it did not give necessary attention to those factors outside the realm of theology (social, political, cultural, psychological etc.) that have often proven to be more serious causes of basic division than purely theological factors. The christological method also had implications for ecclesiology. The trinitarian basis and mystical dimension of the church – elements that had entered gradually into the ecumenical problematic, largely due to the Orthodox contribution[60] – came to be understood wholly in relation to Christ and the founding of the creation, world and church. "The church (or the church communities existing in each place) is the church only when it participates in the work of the trinitarian God in history. The earthly nature of the church and at the same time the churchly nature of the world (or the spiritual nature of the world and the sacredness of creation, as the Orthodox would put it)[61] must not be forgotten."[62] This implied, in other words, that it was impossible to make a case for the unity of the church while being indifferent to the unity of humankind.[63]

In 1968 the fourth assembly of the WCC in Uppsala, Sweden, further developed this trend, although the members of the Faith and Order section had recommended something quite different when they met in Bristol the previous year. The present conflict among the churches, they urged, needed to be seriously examined and seen as a consequence of "differing, however legitimate, interpretations of one and the same gospel".[64] The assembly nevertheless decided instead to propose a "study of the unity of the church within the context of the unity of humankind".[65]

The endorsement of the contextual methodology. At this point, so critical for the continuation of the ecumenical dialogue, we find the experimental use and final adoption of the methodology that came to be labelled *contextual* or *intercontextual*, together with its derivative, *contextual theology*.[66] Every tradition, every theological position and indeed every text is now seen to be connected to a specific setting. "Every text has a context", becomes the characteristic motto.[67] This context is not merely something external to the tradition or theological position or text that simply modifies it, but it is understood instead to constitute an integral part of it. All traditions – especially of "traditional" churches such as the Orthodox – are inseparably linked to a specific historical, sociocultural, political, and even economic and psychological context. This means that theology and tradition are made relative. The traditional data can no longer be used as a rationale for an abstract universal theology that carries absolute and unlimited authority. What takes the place of this is a wide range of theologies appropriate to the multiple varieties of human contexts. At this point we must acknowledge that many factors have helped shape this contextual understanding of theology.

Pluralism – the various contemporary views of humanity, of the world, of the meaning of human experience, and above all of the theological significance of social and cultural context – has had a dramatic influence on the above understanding of theology, on its role, as well as on the method (contextual) with which it is pursued. According to W.A. Visser 't Hooft,[68] *pluralism* – as an ontological fact of contemporary approach to knowledge, and as today's only universal cultural reality and worldview[69] – should not be seen as a negative force in the history of the ecumenical movement but as the sole opportunity for realistically confronting the difficulty of searching for church unity in the midst of a legitimate variety of forms. Pluralism, if not viewed as a tool for relativizing truth, can lead to conceptualizing the church's unity as a "conciliar fellowship of local churches, all different because of their various local contexts, or in other words their various traditions, geographies, cultures, temporal circumstances etc., but all united conciliarly in a common faith and hope in Christ".[70]

Contextual theology and experience. While pluralism is an important aspect of contextual theology, its most prominent feature is the significance it gives to human *experience*. If theology, as K. Pathil points out, is an intellectual concept based on the data of revelation and faith, at the same time it is also a concept of human experience, a concept of the human being as the one who "theologizes", since revelation and faith become tangible realities here and now only in and through human experience. In this way, the human being is not only the subject but also the object of theological reflection; the human being provides not only the context but also the content of theology. This means that no one theology – whether apostolic, patristic, or Byzantine etc. – is capable of being the authentic, self-evident, eternal truth that serves for all time as the reference point in the quest for the unity of the church.[71] The latest period of the ecumenical movement has therefore also witnessed the growing conceptualization of theology as metaphysical anthropology.[72] More and more it is maintained that human experience is both the only approach to the divine and the only safety valve that can check the excesses of theology and keep it healthy. But here too, the obvious variety of human experiences, formed in differing social, cultural, economic, political and psychological contexts, eliminates the very possibility of a single "universal" theology. A given theology is thus transformed into something "local" and "temporal" – or to use the categories of classical or academic theology, into practical theology, or theology of struggle (for liberation, for hope etc.), or theology of spirituality and ascetic life, or liturgical theology and so forth. Thus, all theology becomes "contextual theology".[73] The question posed by contextual theology, in contrast to classical theology, is not so much whether and to what extent the theological positions are in agreement with the tradition, but if these positions have any dynamic reference and relation at all to the given conditions of today's world.

Here is a characteristic example taken from the area of Christian witness. In the earlier ecumenical period the churches were interested in *charitable diakonia*, with concrete expressions that were directed towards the *results* of social indifference and injustice. After some time, an interest in *social diakonia* began to develop within the WCC, and the concrete expressions of that interest likewise shifted towards the *causes* of social indifference and injustice.[74] The change in concrete expression was a function of the change in context.

The same holds true on the purely theological level: nothing can serve as an authoritative basis for dialogue, even if attested by Holy Scripture or church tradition, since every experience of the church is conditioned by a certain (and therefore relative) context. For no contested issue – e.g. the question of the ordination of women, or of inclusive language, or even of the trinitarian basis of Christian faith – does the argument "from tradition" any longer constitute an unshakeable and unchangeable part of contemporary ecumenical dialogue. Contextual theology, taking as its point of departure the certainty that the church is a "sign" of the kingdom of God and of the unity given by the triune God, calls into question the ability of the established institutions to advance on the road towards an egalitarian community of men and women, both within the church and in the society at large.[75] Similar questions might be raised both about the relationship between the eternal and inviolable "gospel" and finite "culture", and even more pointedly about the dialogue of Christianity with other living religions.

Contextual theology and Orthodoxy. The question facing the Orthodox church is how to make the legitimate variety of experiences of other Christian traditions acceptable to all, without sacrificing its theological understanding of the catholicity or completeness of its own ecclesial identity. Furthermore, how can Orthodox theological education remain critically tied to the Orthodox tradition, to the Eastern (Byzantine, cultural, historical etc.) context, without being merely and exclusively a conventional expression of this context? How, in other words, will it acquire globalization, since salvation is certainly global?

Before closing this brief presentation on the leading methodology now being used in the multilateral ecumenical dialogue,[76] and passing over its achievements,[77] I need to emphasize that this method, in spite of its unquestionable benefits, is regularly criticized, mainly for the dangers it poses in practice.[78] I would like to remind you at this point of the accurate observation by the late Nikos Nissiotis that we must not exclude the possibility of a universally and fully authoritative theology, perhaps even on the basis of the transcendent anthropology of contextual theology.[79] Such a prospect suggests possibilities for making corrective adjustments and developments in the basic delineation of the methodology.

* * *

Ecumenism is undoubtedly undergoing a serious and lingering crisis. Many are now speaking of an "ecumenical winter".[80] The presence of the Orthodox in the active work of the WCC is now more than necessary. This responsibility was recently reaffirmed formally, in spite of adverse historical circumstances, by the message from the prelates of Orthodox churches. This presence, however, can be effective and fruitful only on the basis of a common, or at least commonly acceptable, theological methodology. This is precisely the reason for the enormous success of the first stage of the ecumenical dialogue, when Orthodox theology, with the riches of its Eastern patristic inheritance, was instrumental in addressing all issues of major importance. But if at that time the intervention of the Orthodox took place primarily within the Catholic-Protestant dialectical problematic of the urban West, today the Orthodox are obliged to come to terms with the growing and certainly most vibrant section of Christianity – the new churches and Christian groups of the third world that normally use contextual theology. A serious analysis and objective reflection on the relation between Orthodox theology and the contextual theologies without doubt would be helpful and necessary. Significantly, the well-known American feminist theologian Rosemary Ruether acknowledges that "the study of Eastern Orthodoxy with its holistic understanding of nature, grace, the human person and the world continued to be meaningful for all her subsequent reflection and activities".[81] The comment of a colleague of mine in relation to the uproar provoked by the Canberra presentation of Prof. Chung Hyun-Kyung is extremely enlightening for our subject. "It may be that both the Presbyterian theologian and the Orthodox could have entered upon a fruitful dialogue if they had reexamined the teaching of the Orthodox fathers concerning God's continuous self-revelation in creation and history, where – according to Orthodox theology – the Holy Spirit continually gives existence, life, meaning and a share in the divine life (*theosis*) to all created objects and beings, but always according to the corresponding potential of each: the inanimate are given existence; the animate are given existence and life; the rational are given existence, life, meaning and *theosis*."[82]

The Prospects

Can Orthodox theology indeed dialogue with the contextual theologies? Or to put it more boldly: Is Orthodox theology contextual? These questions will continue to require reflection and study. But I have no doubt that a candid dialogue of Orthodox theology, the primary Christian theology "from above", with the various contemporary theologies "from below" that use this particular method will prove to be beneficial to both parties.[83] That is why the Orthodox unceasingly pray for the unity of the church and look forward to the restoration of the broken unity of one body of Christ. All that Orthodoxy can offer to the world is the treasure of its rich past tradition, unbroken over 20 centuries. There is, however, something more. The Orthodox church should witness in the midst of the non-Orthodox its right vision of *communion* and *otherness* (derived from its trinitarian, pneumatological, cosmic and above all eucharistic vision of existence), at a time when communion with the other is becoming extremely difficult, not only outside the Orthodox church, but unfortunately very often inside it.[84] This means that the role of Orthodoxy in regard to ecumenism is neither to proselytize nor to impress and charm with its "exotic" appearance, not even just to witness to its tradition. Its role is to acquire and live communion with the other. As Metropolitan of Pergamon John Zizioulas has emphasized, "This can only happen through a slow process, a *kenotik* presence and a genuine integration. It can only happen in close and creative cooperation and truthful dialogue."[85]

NOTES

[1] Cf. his initiative to call the meeting of all the Orthodox prelates, which resulted in their message reaffirming Orthodoxy's commitment to authentic ecumenism, but also his influential speech in the European Parliament.

[2] More on this decision in all the recent Orthodox newsletters and bulletins. The important session of the Russian synod took place in late 1994.

[3] The recommendations of the official Joint Theological Commission to the respective churches is to proceed to the lifting of all the remaining obstacles that hinder full communion. The corresponding equivalent in Western Christianity is the Porvoo common statement (1992).

[4] According to its constitution, the society's main aims are (1) to promote the dialectic presence of Orthodox theology within the current dialogue for today's problems, cultivate an ecumenical theology, and develop an ecumenical conscience in the Orthodox world; (2) to inform the general public about the situation of the Orthodox churches around the world and to collect all necessary information concerning their ecumenical concerns; (3) to study the development and the problems of the ecumenical dialogue (bilateral as well as multilateral) and to inform the ecclesiastical public about the ecumenical movement; (4) to promote the ecumenicity of Orthodoxy, actively participate in the inter-Orthodox, interchurch, interfaith, and general ecumenical dialogue, by making the necessary theological interventions on any important current issue; and (5) to establish creative relations with all important world ecumenical organizations (World Council of Churches, Conference of European Churches, Pro Oriente, Societas Ecumenica, Kairos etc.) and critically to support all ecumenical initiatives aiming at a peaceful co-existence of the peoples.

[5] S. McCrae Cavert, *The American Churches and the Ecumenical Movement 1895-1961*, Geneva, 1966, p.36.

[6] D.J. Bosch, *Transforming Mission: Paradigm Shifts in Theology of Mission*, New York, 1991, pp.212-13.

[7] V. Lossky, *The Mystical Theology of the Eastern Church*, London, 1957.

[8] Ion Bria, *The Sense of Ecumenical Tradition: The Ecumenical Witness and Vision of the Orthodox*, Geneva, 1991, p.2.

[9] N. Nissiotis, "Interpreting Orthodoxy", *The Ecumenical Review*, 14, 1961, p.26.

[10] Cf. e.g. J. Zizioulas, "The Mystery of the Church in Orthodox Tradition", *One in Christ*, 24, 1988, p.294.

[11] G. Florovsky, "The Elements of Liturgy", in C. Patelos, ed., *The Orthodox Church in the Ecumenical Movement*, Geneva, 1978, p.172.

[12] Here the church is understood as a sign of the kingdom of God, and liturgy as its glimpse and proleptic manifestation. It is important also to note that the Orthodox understanding of the liturgy goes far beyond the ritual; rather, it is an authentic expression of the relation of the people of God to the Creator, to humanity and to the entire cosmos.

[13] Cf., however, P.Tarazi's plea for a "baptismal" theology in his article "The Parish in the New Testament", an address to a recent Syndesmos assembly, published in the *St Vladimir's Theological Quarterly*, 36, 1992.

[14] Cf. the influential contribution of N. Afanassiev, "The Church Which Presides in Love", in *The Primacy of Peter in the Orthodox Church*, collective works by J. Meyendorff, N. Afanassiev, A. Schmemann and N. Kouloumzin, London, 1963, pp.57-110, originally published as "La doctrine de la primauté à la lumière de l'ecclésiologie", *Istina*, 4, 1957, pp.401-20. Further development

of this basic Orthodox teaching, with corrective remarks, appears in J. Zizioulas, *Being as Communion: Studies in Personhood and the Church*, New York, 1985.

[15] Other significant aspects of Orthodox theology include the teaching about the *theotokos*, but they are all consequences of Christology, i.e. of trinitarian theology. That is why the Orthodox have never articulated a "mariology" but have developed a teaching on the "All-Holy *theotokos*" with extremely important anthropological significance (cf. A. Schmemann, *The Presence of Mary*, Santa Barbara, Calif., 1988).

[16] The Orthodox church has never dogmatized a teaching that does not appear in some form in the Bible.

[17] Cf. C. Konstandinidis, "The Significance of the Eastern and Western Traditions within Christendom", in C. Patelos, ed., *The Orthodox Church*, pp.220ff.

[18] G. Florovsky, "Sobornost: The Catholicity of the Church", in E.L. Marschal, ed., *The Church of God*, London, 1934, pp.64-65.

[19] Cf. my "Biblical Consideration of Christian Mission" (in Greek), in Ion Bria and P.Vassiliadis, eds, *Orthodox Christian Witness*, Katerini, 1989, pp.119-40.

[20] *Ibid.*, p.15 from the English original, in I. Bria, ed., *Go Forth in Peace: Orthodox Perspectives on Mission*, Geneva, 1985, p.3.

[21] Vassiliadis, "Biblical Consideration", p.135.

[22] Cf. Zizioulas, *Being as Communion*, pp.209ff.

[23] Cf. T. Stylianopoulos, "The Filioque Dogma: Theologoumenon or Error?", in T. Stylianopoulos and S. Mark Hein, eds, *Spirit of Truth: Ecumenical Perspectives on the Holy Spirit*, Brookline, Mass., 1986, pp.25-80.

[24] For a short explication of this hymn, see G. Lemopoulos, "Come Holy Spirit", *The Ecumenical Review*, 41, 1989, pp.461ff.

[25] Zizioulas, *Being as Communion*, p.140.

[26] Y. Congar, *I Believe in the Holy Spirit*, New York, 1983, vol. 3, p.208, quoted from N. Lossky, *Orthodox Theology*.

[27] Cf. Stylianopoulos, "The Filioque Dogma", p.24.

[28] Cf. P. Vassiliadis, "Episcopacy – Diakonia – Apostleship" (in Greek), in *Biblical Hermeneutical Studies*, Thessaloniki, 1988, pp.364-90.

[29] Zizioulas, *Being as Communion*, p.163.

[30] Zizioulas, "The Mystery", p.400.

[31] Cf. J. Breck, *The Power of the Word in the Worshiping Church*, New York, 1986, for a careful and balanced consideration of the relationship between worship and the gospel.

[32] Zizioulas, "The Mystery", p.302.

[33] Cf. also C. Konstandinidis, "The Significance of the Eastern and Western Traditions within Christendom", in C. Patelos, ed., *The Orthodox Church*, pp.220ff.; Zizioulas, *Being as Communion*, p.26.

[34] One of the most interesting assesments is the article by L. Vischer, "Ist das wirklich die 'Einheit' die wir suchen?", *Ökumenische Rundschau*, 41, 1992, pp.7-24. See the extremely enlightening publication by G. Lemopoulos, *The Seventh Assembly of the WCC: Canberra, February 1991: Chronicle – Documents – Evaluations* (in Greek), Katerini, 1992; also G. Limouris, "The Seventh Assembly of the WCC: Its Theological Problems and the Orthodox Presence and Witness", *Gregorios ho Palamas*, 74, 1991, pp.345ff.

[35] It is tragic that the conflict between the traditional Orthodoxy and the newer churches and theological trends (contextual theologies), which as a rule have taken as their point of departure the dynamics of the third world, has spilled over into the debate on pneumatology per se, which had been something the Orthodox had previously been anticipating so eagerly. See the Orthodox contribution to the subject in "Come Holy Spirit, Renew the Whole Creation", in G. Lemopoulos, ed., *Come Holy Spirit, Renew the Whole Creation* (in Greek), Katerini, 1991, p.188.

[36] See "Reflections of the Orthodox Delegates" (from Canberra) and "The Orthodox Churches and the World Council of Churches" (Chambésy, 12-16 September 1991), *The Seventh Assembly*, pp.77ff., 93ff. respectively (in Greek). Also characteristic are the remarks by Dr Yeow Choo Lak, "After the Seventh Assembly What?", *Ministerial Formation*, 54, 1991, pp.2-6. In his evaluation of Canberra he emphasizes that Professor Chung's presentation "was followed in shrill pursuit by the cry of 'syncretism!' This time, however, the accusation come not from those conservative fundamentalists who without a trace of sensitivity were demonstrating outside the main entrance of the conference centre, but from our Orthodox brothers (I did not hear a single criticism from the Orthodox sisters). I was disappointed by the accusation" (p.3).

[37] Among the studies and assessments of the seventh assembly of the WCC included in the Greek anthology by G. Lemopoulos, the final essay by my colleague from Boston, Fr E. Klapsis, focuses especially on methodology, "What the Spirit Says to the Churches: Implications for Mission of the Seventh Assembly of the WCC" (in Greek), pp.239-64.

[38] See above, n. 36. The Chambésy document is a further rewording of the "Reflections" of Canberra.

[39] See M. Kinnamon and J. Nicole, "The Challenge of Canberra for Theological Education", *Ministerial Formation*, 54, 1991, pp.7ff.

[40] Ion Bria, *The Sense of Ecumenical Tradition: The Ecumenical Witness and Vision of the Orthodox*, Geneva, 1991, pp.46-48.

[41] The only substantial attempt within the Orthodox theological world to address this issue was by N. Nissiotis in his work *The Defence of Hope* (in Greek), Athens, 1975 (first appeared as a series in the journal *Theologia*, 46 [1974], pp.41ff., 273ff., 482ff.). Characteristically, this leading subject in the ecumenical dialogue did not succeed in getting attention at the second conference of Orthodox theological schools, which met in Athens the very next year, in spite of the positive contribution made by N. Nissiotis in his introduction to the main theme of the conference ("Introduction to the Theme of the Second Conference of Orthodox Theological Schools: The Theology of the Church and Its Realization", *Praktika* [Minutes, pp.63-76], p.67). After this genuine introduction, the sole contribution to this theme was by another leading ecumenist of Orthodoxy, Prof. B. Istavridis, "The Ecumenical Dimension of Orthodoxy", *ibid*, (pp.539-56), p.546. See his concluding remarks as well on pp.553ff. See also A. Papadopoulos, *The Witness and Service of Orthodoxy Today* (in Greek), Thessaloniki, 1983, p.86ff.

[42] Cf. the section "Reflections on the Methodology of Faith and Order Study", in the meeting that immediately followed in Accra, Ghana (*Accra – Uniting in Hope: Reports and Documents from the Meeting of the Faith and Order Commission*, 23 July-5 August 1974, University of Ghana, Legon, Faith and Order paper 72, Geneva, pp.66-82). Cf. also Choan-Seng Song, ed., *Doing Theology Today*, Madras, 1976, together with the minutes of the above Bossey conferences, where there is a considerable Orthodox contribution by N. Nissiotis entitled "Ecclesial Theology in Context", pp.101-24. Cf. also the special issue of *Study Encounter*, vol. 8, no. 3, 1972; also M. Begzos, "'The Account of Hope': The Report of the "Faith and Order" Conference of the WCC" (in Greek), *Ekklesia*, 57, 1980, pp.58ff.,85ff.

[43] Lukas Vischer very rightly notes that while each stage of the dialogue is marked by a specific methodology, the various methodologies have continued to co-exist. He makes this point in the prologue to Kuncheria Pathil's relevant work *Models in Ecumenical Dialogue: A Study of the Methodological Development in the Commission on "Faith and Order" of the World Council of Churches*, Bangalore, 1981, pp.xiiiff.

[44] See the working papers of the Louvain conference, perhaps the sole meeting in the history of the WCC not to publish official reports, from John Deschner, *Faith and Order Louvain 1971: Study, Reports and Documents*, Geneva, 1971, pp.184-99.

[45] There is tragic irony in the fact that the Louvain conference almost led to a break because of the Orthodox presence, specifically with the presidential address of the then head of the Faith and Order commission, the late Fr John Meyendorff, who was one of the leading Orthodox theologians and pioneers in the ecumenical dialogue. And now, over 20 years later, with the initiative of an Orthodox theological institution (the theological faculty of the University of Thessaloniki), an attempt is being made to elucidate the relationship between Orthodox theology and the nearly dominant thelogical methodology within the WCC.

[46] Another critical moment was in 1961 at the third assembly of the WCC in New Delhi, when the basis of the charter of the WCC was changed from christological to trinitarian and the entirety of Orthodoxy officially entered the WCC.

[47] See the interesting article by the Russian theologian Fr Vitaly Borovoy, "The Ecclesiastical Significance of the WCC: The Legacy and Promise of Toronto", in *Commemorating Amsterdam 1948: 40 Years of the WCC* (= *The Ecumenical Review*, 40, 1988, pp.504-18).

[48] A characteristic example is the document *Common Witness* (by the Joint Working Group of the Roman Catholic Church and the World Council of Churches), Geneva, 1981; also, the importance of *Baptism, Eucharist and Ministry*, a purely theological document also with participation of the Roman Catholic Church, cannot be overestimated.

[49] Bria, *The Sense of Ecumenical Tradition*, p.25. See also Papadopoulos, *Witness and Service*, pp.126ff.

50 As far as Orthodox theology is concerned, there have been a number of meetings at which the ecumenical perspective of Orthodoxy was upheld (1972 in Thessaloniki, the regular gatherings of the Orthodox Theological Society of America, the second conference of Orthodox theologians in 1976).

51 What is known as the New Valaamo report forms also the basis for the resolution "The Orthodox Church and the Ecumenical Movement" of the third pan-Orthodox preconciliar consultation.

52 This method was used mainly during the Faith and Order consultations prior to the founding of the WCC (Geneva 1920, Lausanne 1927, Edinburgh 1937) and continued as well in subsequent theological policies of the WCC. See Pathil, *Models in Ecumenical Dialogue*, pp.247ff.

53 In ecumenical circles the method is known as Barthian dialectics and is often associated with his views.

54 On this subject see my studies "Orthodoxy and the West" and "Orthodox Theology on the Threshold of the 21st Century", in *Orthodoxy at the Crossroads* (in Greek), Thessaloniki, 1992, pp.91ff. and 35ff. respectively.

55 For this reason it is also known in later documents as the Lund method or Lund methodology (Pathil, *Models in Ecumenical Dialogue*, p.314, n. 1).

56 T.F. Torrance, *Conflict and Agreement in the Church*, vol. 1, Naperville, Ill., 1959, p.202.

57 Among the classic achievements of the period are the affirmations that unity is not our own hypothesis but a given fact of the Holy Spirit, the church as "event" and not institution, the predominance of the "body of Christ" view of the church's identity etc.

58 It was not only New Testament scholars who pointed out the ecclesiological diversity of the New Testament. See the much-discussed introduction by E. Käsemann at the fourth international conference of the section on Faith and Order, Montreal, 1963, on the theme "Unity and Diversity in New Testament Ecclesiology", *Novum Testamentum*, 6, 1963, pp.290ff. and the discussion following; other points of view, particularly the Anglo-Saxon, criticized the excessively meta-historical character of his views, which gradually came to dominate all theological discussion, as if the churches were located outside this world.

59 Orthodox criticism and recollection of this lost perspective was almost a monotonous refrain of the Orthodox representatives, even after the trinitarian broadening of the foundation of the WCC's charter. But it was especially vocal when "monistic Christology" was the order of the day.

60 Typical are the observations of J.B. Torrance, in contrast to those of the introducers of christological method into the ecumenical dialogue. This celebrated Scottish theologian asked why the dogma of the Holy Trinity "has so often receded from being central in the thinking of our Western churches", J. B. Torrance, "The Doctrine of the Trinity in Our Contemporary Situation", in A.I.C. Heron, ed., *The Forgotten Trinity*, London, 1991, p.3.

61 According to N. Matsoukas, *The Ecumenical Movement: History-Theology* (in Greek), Thessaloniki, 1986, "the entire creation is inviolably sacred" (p.19). See also his work *World, Man, and Society according to Maximus the Confessor* (in Greek), Athens, 1980.

62 Pathil, *Models in Ecumenical Dialogue*, p.345.

63 See C. Yannaras, *The Unity of the Church and the Unity of Humankind* (in Greek), Athens, 1972.

64 See *New Directions in Faith and Order: Bristol 1967. Reports – Minutes – Documents*, Geneva, 1968, p.41.

65 Significantly, the minutes of the Uppsala consultation were published with the title *Unity of Mankind*, Geneva, 1969. For this reason also in 1971 the meeting in Louvain – where for the first time this method met with success – had as its main theme "Unity of the Church – Unity of Mankind".

66 "Theologizing in context", as it was termed by the late Nikos Nissiotis in the only Greek reference that treats this subject systematically (cf. his *The Defence of Hope*). Classical theology, in contrast, is associated in ecumenical circles with theological work that depended more or less on the earlier methodologies.

67 Pathil, *Models in Ecumenical Dialogue*, p.346.

68 "Pluralism – Temptation or Opportunity?" *The Ecumenical Review*, 1966, pp.129-49.

69 Cf. two very interesting studies by B. Lonergan: *Doctrinal Pluralism*, Milwaukee, 1971; and *Method in Theology*, New York, 1972.

70 Today, when eucharistic theology is almost the universal reference point in the ecumenical dialogue, the optimism of Visser 't Hooft's view is considered insufficient and has been overtaken by reality. See also A. Osipov, "The Ecumenicity of Orthodoxy" (in Greek), *Praktika*, p.538, but also the elucidation by T. Sabev, who calls for "real fraternal communion within the Orthodox church and a limited unity (fellowship) between us and the other churches" (Response 1 [in Greek] to the above paper, *Praktika*, p.533.

[71] Pathil, *Models in Ecumenical Dialogue*, pp.363-64. According to N. Matsoukas, the Orthodox tradition includes a dual theological methodology. In the first, the human being comes to know the uncreated God and the related mystery in the vision of God, in the direct vision of the divine glory; in the second method, knowledge approaches knowledge of all-created reality through science. See his recent introduction to the Inter-Christian Symposium of the Theological Faculty and the Ateneum Antonianum Spirituality Institute of Rome on the theme of the vision of God and prayer, entitled "The Theophanies in the History of Israel and the Church as Sources of the Vision and Knowledge of God" (in Greek), in *Antipelargesis: Essays in Honor of Archbishop Chrysostom of Cyprus on the 25th Anniversary of His Episcopal Service*, Lefkosia, 1993, pp.323-31; and also his two-volume work *Dogmatic and Symbolic Theology* (in Greek), Thessaloniki, 1985, vol. 1, pp.181ff.

[72] Cf. K. Rahner, E. Schillebeeckx and others. See T. Patrick Burke, ed., *The Word in History*, New York, 1966.

[73] Within Orthodoxy something analogous is the discovery of an authentic "liturgical theology". In addition, at the Faith and Order conference in Lund (1952) it was emphasized officially by the Orthodox that "Christianity is a liturgical religion. The church is above all a worshiping community. Worship comes first, doctrine and discipline second. The lex orandi (the rule of prayer) has priority in the life of the Christian church. The lex credendi (the rule of faith) proceeds from the worshiping experience and vision of the church" (G. Florovsky, "Orthodox Worship", in *Themes of Orthodox Theology*, Greek translation 1973, p.159).

[74] In this way, programmes like PCR developed in opposition to racism, JPIC for justice, peace and the integrity of creation etc.

[75] E.g., "The Ecumenical Decade 1988-1998. The Churches in Solidarity with Women".

[76] See also K.P.Blaser, "Kontextuelle Theologie vor und nach Nairobi", *Zeitschrift für Mission*, 3, 1977, pp.7-23.

[77] A number of developments could be mentioned, e.g. the axiom "unity in diversity", the subsequent trinitarian – and pneumatological – motto of the Council, the elevation of the concept of communion within ecclesiology, the quest for a broader application of an understanding of the "people of God", the greater sensitivity to the mystical character of the church and the necessity of restoring it, the quest for unity as interconnected with the unity of humanity as mentioned above (for a purely Orthodox perspective on this question, see Nissiotis, *The Defence of Hope*), and others.

[78] The Asian Roman Catholic ecumenist Prof. Kuncheria Pathil, who is especially concerned with this subject and is an ardent advocate of the methodology of contextual theology, summarizes the dangers as follows: (1) the complete negation of authentic criteria in the search for the truth contains the danger that each local context and experience could be considered uncritically as an authentic expression of the Christian faith; (2) the relativity and transience of contextual theology can be a temptation to underestimate eternal and universal truths such as human finitude, sin etc.; (3) with the use of other disciplines by contextual theology, it is very easy for theology to escape into the philosophy or sociology or psychology etc. of religion; (Pathil, *Models in Ecumenical Dialogue*, pp.393ff); see also the studies of Konrad Raiser, *Identität und Sozialität*, Munich, 1971, and *Ecumenism in Transition*, Geneva, 1991.

[79] Nissiotis, "Ecclesial Theology in Context", p.124.

[80] Anton Houtepen in the inaugural presidential address of the seventh conference of the Societas Oecumenica (Salamanca 1992), in which the recently elected general secretary of the WCC, Konrad Raiser, refers to "mounting confessionalism and ecclesiotribalism".

[81] R.R. Ruether, *Disputed Questions*, New York, 1984, p.37.

[82] Matsoukas, "The Theophanies in the History of Israel", p.330.

[83] This was the conclusion of the symposium jointly organized by the department of theology of the University of Thessaloniki and the Ecumenical Institute of Bossey, in Thessaloniki (2-3 October 1992), on the subject "Classical Theology and Contextual Theology: The Role of Orthodox Theology in the Post-Canberra Ecumenical Movement".

[84] In a recent paper entitled "Communion and Otherness", delivered at the eighth Orthodox congress in Western Europe, Blankenberge, Belgium, 29 October-1 November 1993, J. Zizioulas argued that "individual Orthodox Christians may fail... but the church as a whole should not.... When the 'other' is rejected on account of natural, sexual, racial, social, ethic or even moral – in other words contextual – differences, Orthodox witness is destroyed".

[85] *Ibid.*

3. Mission and Proselytism:
An Orthodox Understanding

My goal here is to provide an Orthodox understanding of the burning issue of proselytism within the ecumenical movement and its relation to the Christian imperative of mission. Our context is today's outburst of missionary and/or proselytizing activities from various Christian quarters, with or without real and authentic evangelistic awareness. I begin with a few preliminary remarks.

I do not intend here to widen the diversity that already exists among member churches of the WCC with regard to the theological concept of mission, which as I will try to show later is the real cause of the still unresolved problem of proselytism within Christianity of our time, more precisely within the WCC. I propose, therefore, not to expound a strictly "confessional" (i.e. Orthodox) point of view, but what I understand of the "one, holy, catholic and apostolic church" – in other words, what the ecclesially and ecumenically "Orthodox" approach to mission and proselytism should be, as enriched by my ecclesial (i.e. liturgical) and evangelistic (i.e. martyria) experience.

The views expressed in this study therefore do not represent, and cannot claim to be, the official Orthodox understanding – on the contrary, I have recently been quite critical of it[1] – but they are strictly my own. This is quite obvious for both historical and theological reasons. For the former, because the secular contexts within which Orthodox eucharistic communities scattered around the world give their witness and make their individual approaches to mission are incredibly varied. (The range includes established/metropolitan churches, diaspora and/or Western Orthodox churches, new/missionary churches, as well as "traditional" Orthodox churches that have suffered during the past generations because of a lack of liberty.) For the latter, because in our Eastern tradition, by far the more consistent in the trinitarian (i.e. pneumatological)

• An earlier version of this chapter appeared in *International Review of Mission*, 85, 1996, pp. 257-75.

understanding of the church, we firmly believe in the diversity of the charismata of the Holy Spirit.

My approach to the subject will be neither strictly historical nor purely confessional but theological and ecumenical (i.e. critical, and sometimes even self-critical).[2] After all, the real function of theology is to be the critical conscience of the church. In addition, I propose not to refer in detail to the various agreed ecumenical statements on proselytism, the various arguments of both sides,[3] or the various legitimate and justified complaints by the Orthodox church, which has been the most affected in the last two centuries by this caricature of authentic evangelism.[4]

Orthodoxy needs to reaffirm its commitment to ecumenism if it expects a lasting solution to this issue of proselytism, which is most painful in the present circumstances. I stress this point because it is a widespread conviction nowadays that ecumenism has entered a delicate and crucial stage, with the signs of a decline clearly in evidence. The tragic events we experienced since the great changes in Europe – including churches not being in solidarity with, but fighting or undermining, each other; and with nations and peoples not desiring to live peacefully with others but wishing to "cleanse" them – are indications that the titanic ecumenical efforts of the past definitely need reorientation.

I

In order properly to tackle the issue of proselytism, one needs to examine a variety of terms and notions involved in current ecumenical discussions, expressed by such words as *mission, conversion, evangelism* or *evangelization, Christianization, witness* and *martyria*. Of these terms only the last two have been widely adopted in ecumenical circles as the more appropriate for a genuine and authentic Christian mission,[5] whereas those belonging to the "evangelical" stream of our Christian tradition have retained all the others as the sine qua non of Christian identity.[6]

In his recent book *Mission and Conversion: Proselytizing in the Religious History of the Roman Empire*, Martin Goodman has discerned four different uses of the word "mission" in modern scholarship of the history of religions, and consequently four different understandings of what has come to be labeled as "Christian mission":

The informative mission. The missionaries of this type felt "that they had a general message which they wished to impart to others. Such disseminators of information may have had no clear idea of the reaction they desired from their auditors.... [The aim of this attitude] was to tell people something, rather than to change their behaviour or status."[7] Of this type was the mission of the first evangelist women who announced the good news of Christ's resurrection, the prime event of the Christian faith.

The educational mission. "Some missionaries did intend to change recipients of their message by making them more moral or contented.... Such a mission to educate is easily distinguished from a desire to win converts."[8] The first monastics, regardless of their motivation in beginning their movement, exercised this type of mission.

The apologetic mission. "Some missionaries requested recognition by others of the power of a particular divinity without expecting their audience to devote themselves to his or her worship. Such a mission was essentially apologetic. Its aim was to protect the cult and beliefs of the missionary."[9] Obviously, the early Christian apologists belonged to this type of missionaries.

The proselytizing mission. According to Goodman, "Information, education, and apologetic might or might not coexist within any one religious system, but all three can individually be distinguished from what may best be described as proselytizing... [the aim of which was] to encourage outsiders not only to change their way of life but also to be incorporated within their group."[10] No doubt this last type of mission, for which the terms "conversion" and "Christianization" seem to apply better, was the ideal behind the universal proselytizing mission of modern times. The origins of this type of mission can be traced back to St Paul (though in scholarly circles this is still debated) and to the dominical saying recorded at the end of St Matthew's gospel (28:18b-20).

This pluralistic understanding of Christian mission in the history of the early church, apostolic and post-apostolic alike, has undoubtedly given place more or less to a universalistic understanding in the form of a universal proselytizing mission that during the Constantinian period became dominant through its theological validation by the great church historian Eusebius. However, it never became entirely dominant in the undivided church,[11] at least in the Eastern Orthodox church, with very few exceptions.

It does not concern us here whether this understanding of the universal proselytizing mission is to be explained on theological grounds (i.e. as a straightforward result of the high Christology of the early Christian/Pauline recapitulation-in-Christ theory) or on grounds of cultural anthropology (i.e. as a legitimate demand within the Roman empire after

Constantine the Great for the ideal of "uniformity within a given society"). It will suffice to note that the eventual Christianization of the Roman empire inevitably had a significant effect on the future of our Western world, and to a considerable degree it has also determined in later times the shape of the Western theology of mission, Catholic and Protestant alike.[12] The issue of a universal proselytizing mission in Western Christianity, in fact, was given fresh life by the discovery of the New World and by the prospect of Christianizing the entire inhabited earth. It reached its peak with the African and Asian missions during the last century.[13] This concept of "Christendom", however, carried with it other non-Christian elements to such an extent that eventually industrialized development in Europe and America of the bourgeois society as well as colonialism walked hand in hand with Christian mission.

In his fascinating book *Ecumenism in Transition: A Paradigm Shift in the Ecumenical Movement*, Konrad Raiser has rightly pointed out that Christians at the "old ecumenical paradigm" felt that they were called

> to convey to the rest of humanity the blessings of Western (i.e. bourgeois) Christian civilization.... The slogan "the evangelization of the world in this generation" emphasizes the missionary consciousness of this early movement, in which genuine missionary and evangelistic motives were inextricably combined with cultural and social motives.[14]

Raiser, however, suggested for the future of ecumenism and of Christian mission a radical shift to a new paradigm, away from "christocentric universalism" and towards a trinitarian understanding of the divine reality and towards an oikoumene as the one household of life.[15] For the understanding of mission, these concepts mean the abandonment of any effort to proselytize, not only among Christians of other denominations but even among peoples of other religions. *Dialogue* is the new term that now runs parallel to, and in some cases in place of, the old missiological terminology.[16] This development by no means implies that there has been a shift in Christian soteriology from the slogan "No salvation but through Christ"[17] – overcoming the traditional catholic view *extra ecclesiam salus non est*, first expressed by Cyprian of Carthage and later misinterpreted to mean exclusively the institutional (Catholic?) church – to the novel one of "No salvation but through God".[18] Rather, it is a radical reinterpretation of Christology through pneumatology,[19] through the rediscovery of the forgotten trinitarian theology of the undivided church.[20]

In ecumenical circles, therefore, the understanding of mission on theological grounds is moving away from the concept of a universal proselytizing mission. This is due not only to the failure to convert the entire inhabited world or to the disillusion and disappointment caused by the end of the China mission, the most ambitious missionary enterprise in modern Christian missionary history. It was due, rather, to the rediscovery of the authentic identity of the church through the invaluable help of the theological treasures of Orthodoxy. More particularly, it was the result of the reinforcement of pneumatology in ecumenical reflections.[21] It is my firm conviction that the revival of proselytism by certain evangelical groups outside, but also within, the WCC is not so much the result of historical circumstances (such as the collapse of totalitarian regimes, in particular in Central and Eastern Europe) as it is a conscious reaction to the "openness" of the church to the outside world, especially after the latest developments in the ecumenical movement by the more traditional (some may label them even "fundamentalist") segments of Christianity. These segments mainly belong to Protestantism, but they can also be found in Catholicism (cf. e.g. the issue of uniatism, or the very narrow interpretation of the bishops' recent appeal for "re-evangelization" of Europe) and undoubtedly even within Orthodoxy (the Old Calendarists and other traditional groups e.g. are the most active in proselytizing among Western Christian churches and denominations and react the strongest against interfaith dialogue). To some extent it is also due to the still-unresolved tension within the WCC with regard to its stance towards the other religions. If this is so, and the revival of proselytism is an attempt to reverse the understanding and practice of Christian mission, then the problem of proselytism is to be addressed by a thorough reconsideration of the discipline of mission, perhaps through a widely agreed new charter.[22]

Since, however, most of the argument, especially by those of the evangelical stream of our Christian tradition, is still elaborated through the fundamental classical biblical references, I will now turn to them. Through a theological reflection (Orthodox, in the sense I indicated above) on the basic biblical references, I will try to tackle our subject with my limited resources as thoroughly as possible.

II

For hundreds of years the European churches have based their mission on our Lord's demand at the very end of his earthly ministry, as this demand was written down in the well-known Matthaean passage:

> All authority in heaven and on earth has been given to me. Go therefore and
> make disciples of all nations, baptizing them in the name of the Father and of
> the Son and of the Holy Spirit, and teaching them to obey everything that I
> have commanded you. And remember, I am with you always, to the end of the
> age. (Matt. 28:18-20)

The centrality of this passage in the theological foundation of the
European churches' mission was to some extent due to the over-estima-
tion during the pre-critical era of the gospel of Matthew (which was for
some time considered *the* gospel of the church) at the expense of the
fourfold gospel. Furthermore, the place of this important missionary
statement at the very end of Jesus' earthly ministry was interpreted as
inaugurating the close of one era, that of Jesus' mission, and the start of
another, that of human mission. Only under such circumstances can one
explain the widely accepted, but at the same time one-sided, consideration of this otherwise important biblical passage. As a consequence, an
undue emphasis was given to the individualistic and anthropocentric
understanding of "making disciples". As a result, our Christian mission
adopted an expansionist attitude in the past, and in some places, imperialistic tendencies also found their way in, thus eroding the spiritual character of the churches' mission. In addition, our scandalous divisions have
resulted in a denominational antagonism, which in turn has led to proselytizing attitudes transplanting the old-fashioned theological debates
and practices from Europe to non-European missionary areas.

It would have been otherwise, however, had the *trinitarian dimension* of the church's mission been emphasized. The making of disciples
is meaningless without a reference to "baptizing them in the name of the
Father and of the Son and of the Holy Spirit". After all, the call of the
church to mission is rooted in the fact that Christ himself was sent by the
Father, in the Holy Spirit. "As the Father has sent me, so I send you....
Receive the Holy Spirit" (John 20:21-22). And going a little further: the
sending of Christ was the inevitable consequence of the inner dynamics
of the Holy Trinity. In fact, Christian mission can be justified only if we
conceive our missionary task as the projection in human terms of the life
of communion that exists within the Holy Trinity. That is why the subject of mission is not the individual believer, the missionary or even the
church as an impersonal corporate entity – rather, it is the triune God.
Humanity enters into the missionary field only within the framework of
the divine *synergia*. This idea, which the fathers strongly emphasized,
does not mean that we are equal partners with God himself or that he

cannot act independently of humankind, even in the form of the "little flock"; rather, it means that our triune God in his divine economy has consciously decided to work through us. According to Ion Bria,

> Trinitarian theology points to the fact that God is in God's own self a life of communion and that God's involvement in history aims at drawing humanity and creation in general into this communion with God's very life. The implications of this assertion for understanding mission are very important: mission does not aim primarily at the propagation or transmission of intellectual convictions, doctrines, moral commands, etc., but at the transmission of the life of communion that exists in God.[23]

Coming back to our Matthaean passage, we need to note several points.

1. The entire scene of Jesus' sending out his disciples is clearly set within the framework of the resurrection-event. This obvious setting is repeatedly emphasized in our biblical commentaries; its consequences, however, have scarcely been drawn to the extent they deserve. We are called to give our evangelistic witness to the world not as a continuation of the kerygma of Jesus of Nazareth but in the light of a deep understanding and experience of the resurrection of Christ. Our vocation, therefore, is not to propagate religious ideas or to establish religious sects but to reveal Jesus Christ as the Lord and to introduce into the world the reality of his kingdom. It is for this reason that every Sunday, when we meet to worship Christ in the eucharistic gathering, we celebrate the day of resurrection. We can become quite clear indeed about the task facing our churches (thinking particularly of those within the WCC) if we now conceive this eucharistic liturgy as we should, not only as the springboard for mission, but as the missionary event par excellence; not only as the true expression of the divine revelation, but also as a living anticipation of the kingdom to come; not only as a means of perfection of individuals, but also and primarily as a means of the transformation of the church as a community into an authentic image of the kingdom of God, and through the church of the entire cosmos, "so that [by our light shining before others] they may see [our] good works and give glory to [our] Father in heaven" (Matt. 5:16).

2. The sending out of Jesus' disciples is preceded in our text by a solemn declaration that the resurrected Christ is invested with full authority: "All authority in heaven and on earth has been given to me." Throughout the history of patristic interpretation this verse was understood against the background of the incarnation (cf. e.g. Basil the Great).

Actually the authority that Jesus Christ acquired was not bestowed but recovered (*epanadromē, epanalēpsis* [a return, a resumption], according to Cyril of Alexandria). This means that there is perfect harmony between the lordship of Christ and his presence in the world. From the biblical and the apostolic period and throughout the history of the undivided church, our forefathers (and silently our foremothers too) constantly fought against any overemphasis of either the divinity or the humanity of Christ. The meaning of the church's resistance against Docetism, Gnosticism and all the heresies and theological issues that were settled in the ecumenical councils was its conviction that Christ remains wholly *transcendent* to, but at the same time *immanent* and present in, the world. The Matthaean passage that we have discussed presents this truth in a perfectly balanced way. Alongside the reference to Christ's transcendent authority we read his assurance: "and remember, I am with you always." Thus, the transcendent and resurrected Christ is made the motive force of mission in the world. Transcendence without immanence leads inevitably to secularization of the world, depriving the world of its holiness, acquired through the creation, incarnation and re-creation (*anadēmiourgia*), and reducing it to its purely material aspect. We are led to a similar distortion if we emphasize Jesus' immanence without giving due attention to his transcendence. The consequences of such a Christology will result in the impoverishment of the prophetic meaning of the church, reducing it to a mere social movement. In addition, therefore, to the resurrectional aspect, the incarnational aspect is of the greatest importance for the church's mission.

3. Recent historical-critical research is almost unanimous in its conclusion that our Lord's demand "go forth and make disciples of all nations" at the end of St Matthew's gospel is a later product that came out of the resurrectional and pentecostal experience of the early Christian community. It represents the ideal of universal mission that was the result of the success of the Gentile mission, also expressed in other indirect references of the synoptic tradition (Mark 13:10; 14:9 etc.), which nevertheless contradicts the exclusive mission to the Jews practised in the earthly ministry of Jesus (cf. Matt. 15:24). This seeming differentiation from our Lord's mission is nevertheless misleading. For it is quite apparent that the missionary statements and discourses of Jesus in the earliest strata of the gospel tradition (Mark 6:7-13; Matt. 9:37-38; Luke 9:1-6; 10:1-16) have a clear eschatological meaning. The "harvest time" metaphor, which is so often alluded to in the gospels, is in fact in accordance with, or more precisely a reinterpretation of, the Old Testament and

later apocalyptic eschatological pictures (cf. Joel 3:13 [4:13 LXX]; Micah 4:12-13; Isa. 27:12; 2 Apoc. Bar. 70:2, 4; Ezra 4:28-32). In all New Testament contexts the overall mission is therefore an *eschatological* event and should be viewed and practised as such by the church. It is not accidental that St Paul, the greatest missionary of all, was waiting for the kingdom to appear in the near future, yet he made and accomplished far-reaching plans for evangelizing the entire Greco-Roman world. This eschatological perspective, implicitly or explicitly considering the eschaton as an imminent event or fully projected into the present, is dominant to a greater or lesser degree throughout the entire New Testament. And this is clearly echoed in the concluding reference to "the end of the age" of our Matthaean passage (28:20). If we therefore consider the word "nation" in such an eschatological perspective, the thorny question of the relationship between gospel and culture becomes in effect marginal. The multiplicity of ethnic, cultural, linguistic, religious etc. diversities of the world is valued and accepted as such; to a much greater degree, of course, so is the plurality of Christian expressions of faith – provided that the final target always remains the transfiguration of the entire cosmos, humankind and nature alike, into the original beauty and harmony that not only existed before the fall but, to a much greater degree, will be acquired at the eschaton.[24] This is the real meaning of the lordship of Christ, who at the end "will also be subjected to [God] who put all things in subjection under him, so that God may be all in all" (1 Cor. 15:28).

4. The meaning, therefore, of the universal mission assigned by Christ to his disciples by virtue of his unlimited authority, as we described it above (i.e. as a projection of the communion of the Holy Trinity), takes the form of two distinct, but at the same time inter-related, actions: (1) "baptizing" the world, in fact each one personally, "in the name" of the triune God; (2) "teaching" them "to obey" all of Christ's commandments. Both actions point to the kingdom of God. Baptism is a rite of initiation; more precisely it is the sacramental act of entering into the church, the little flock that will transform the entire world into the kingdom of God, exactly as "a little yeast leavens the whole batch of dough" (1 Cor. 5:6). In a similar way, "teaching everything that [Christ has] commanded you" does not aim at establishing a new law by transmission of doctrinal or moral values but primarily has in view a new covenant. The phrase "teaching them to observe all that I have commanded you" echoes St Matthew's habitual presentation of Jesus as the new Moses of the new Israel. Even in the Old Testament (especially in

Deuteronomy), God's commandments are inextricably bound with – in fact they stand as a consequence of – the covenant that God himself in his initiative established with his chosen people (see ch. 7 below).

It is not accidental that in the Lord's prayer the petition "Your will be done" follows the previous fundamental petition: "Your kingdom come." In the New Testament, therefore, God's will for his church, the new Israel, is related to God's new covenant, being in fact identified with the realization and manifestation of the kingdom of God. And for the church there can be no other will of God than the coming of his kingdom, no universal proselytizing mission but proleptic manifestations of God's coming kingdom, beyond cultural, confessional, or even religious boundaries.[25]

These sacramental and covenantal aspects, which both point to the kingdom of God, should never be lost from the missionary perspectives of the church. After all, true evangelism is not aiming at bringing the nations into our religious "enclosure", but seeks to "let" the Holy Spirit use both us and those to whom we bear witness to bring about the kingdom of God. This means that in the church's mission priority should definitely be given not to "quantity" conversions but to the "quality" and exclusiveness of the kingdom of God – or to use K. Raiser's new paradigm, of the household (*oikos*) of God.[26]

III

After the great schism and the eventual split between Eastern and Western Christianity, which seriously wounded the oneness of the church, European theology developed a scholastic system in isolation from its trinitarian basis and developed, perhaps unconsciously, a distorted notion of christocentricity. This was the case, for example, with soteriology, whether or not it goes back to the Anselmian "satisfaction theory". Its classic expression with the *extra nos – pro nobis* formula, which resulted in the passive role the European churches have played in socio-politico-economic development, leaving thus an indelible mark on Western civilization and culture, was in fact due to the transference of the decisive point of salvation from incarnation and the whole of divine economy to the specific moment of Jesus' death on the cross. As a consequence, soteriology (as all the other "-ologies" of Christian theology, including missiology) gradually shifted away from Christology, viewed always within a trinitarian perspective, and eventually became a separate

chapter of (denominational, of course, and not ecclesial) dogmatic theology. However, this was not the way the early, undivided church used to consider soteriology. Our church fathers answered the question of salvation in close relation to – in fact as a consequence of – the Christian doctrine of the nature, essence and energies of the second person of the Holy Trinity.

By losing the trinitarian dimension in the understanding of Christian mission, we lost the holistic and cosmic dimension of salvation, which is clearly implied in the advanced christological statement of the *corpus paulinum*:

> For in him [Christ] all the fullness of God was pleased to dwell, and through him God was pleased to reconcile to himself all things, whether on earth or in heaven, by making peace through the blood of his cross. (Col 1:19-20)

Only a few remarks need to be made on this passage:

1. In all religions except Christianity, the concept of deity is an abstract one; God is the great unknown, whom no one has ever seen face to face. He therefore cannot be classified with existing things because he is above existence itself. Christianity, in contrast, believes that God revealed himself to the world through Christ, the means of revelation being Christ's incarnation, namely the act of his taking flesh. Christ is therefore the actual door through which human beings enter in to the knowledge of God ("whoever has seen me has seen the Father," John 14:9). He is the authentic "image of the invisible God", the Father, "for in him all the fullness of God was pleased to dwell" (Col. 1:15, 19). This truth is perfectly demonstrated by the Greek letters O ΩN (the Existing One) in the Orthodox icons of Christ. In the Christian East the icon of Christ is an icon of God. By seeing the image, we are aware of what is revealed. Without denying the historical-critical views on the origin of the Greek word *plērōma* (fullness), we must remind ourselves of its identification in the patristic exegetical tradition "to the essence and not to a certain energy of God" (Theophylact). Even the view of Theodoret (who on the basis of the parallel Eph. 1:23 and not of the more relevant Col. 2:9 has related the fullness to the church) has something to say: the fullness of God in Christ is shared with the church, thus affecting the whole creation.

2. The reference to reconciliation "through the blood of his cross" no doubt has soteriological connotations. Recent New Testament scholarship is almost unanimous in its opinion that St Paul's understanding of salvation was not an evolution *ex nihilo* but a development and reinterpretation

of the early (pre-Pauline) church's considerable variety of attempts to give a theological interpretation to Jesus' death. Our great apostle preserves, and to a certain extent he accepts all the traditional interpretations, but without showing his preference for any of them. A quick glance at the terminology used by him shows his real contribution to early Christian soteriology. There may be some objections as to the real meaning of the ransom terminology (cf. *apolytrōsis* in Col 1:14) or of the conciliatory (cf. *apokatallaxai* in Col 1:20) or juridical (*dikaios, dikaioun* etc.) terminology, with which the mystery of salvation is expressed in the Pauline epistles, or whether it comes from St Paul himself or expresses the faith of the first Christian community. What no one can deny is that the theological meaning attached to *stauros* (cross) and its cognates constitutes one of the most characteristic features of St Paul's theology. The "word of the cross" became for St Paul the decisive parameter that gave new perspective to the traditional understanding of Jesus' death. And this new perspective is determined by the meaning this form of capital punishment had in the pre-Christian era. It was St Paul who transformed this most terrible, disgracing and humiliating symbol of Roman society into the most significant element in the divine economy. More precisely, while accepting the traditional pluralistic interpretations of this greatest event of the earthly ministry of our Lord, any time his opponents challenged his gospel, he reinterpreted the significance of Jesus' death on the basis of his *theologia crucis*, with all the socio-political consequences this humiliating symbol connoted in contemporary Roman society.

If St Paul's soteriology, the quintessence of our Christian dogmatic theology, has such sociological connotations, we realize what the task of our mission must be. Such an understanding of Christian soteriology would never allow us to be trapped in dilemmas between faith and science in a world facing ecological extinction and genetic manipulation, or between individualistic spirituality and social responsibility in a society controlled by an unjust global economic system and facing a nuclear panic and AIDS epidemic. It teaches us that the Christian church should never lose its social and cosmic dimension and become a privatized religion of individual or even denominational interest.

3. Of similar importance is the use in our passage of the *hapaxlegomenon eirēnopoiēsas* (making peace). It expresses the consequence of the cosmic effect of God's power working in Christ and in his body, the church. It is neither a Stoic idea, according to which peace can be restored if one achieves harmony with one's inner nature, nor is it a political idea of the type of the externally forced pax Romana. It is Christ's

sovereignty over the entire cosmos, the cause, source and manifestation (in concrete actions of his body, the church) of real peace. As is clearly shown in our passage, there is also a sharp contrast with its contemporary Jewish apocalyptic view that shalom (peace) will be restored only at the eschaton. Unlike the apocalyptic literature, in the New Testament, especially in Revelation, peace and final salvation are not envisaged as the once-and-for-all event of the cosmic transformation at the eschaton, but in the specific historical event of the inauguration of the kingdom of God and the subsequent efforts of the church as the authentic manifestation of that kingdom to overthrow all contemporary faithlessness and injustice. It is firmly believed that God's people, despite all difficulties, at the end "will reign on earth" (Rev. 5:10).

This is not naive millenarianism but an affirmation of the church's eschatological (i.e. historical) perspective and an attempt to prevent the Christian understanding of salvation from becoming an illusion or being limited only to the spiritual life, as the Gnostics attempted to do (cf. the gospel of Thomas). Only when Satan and his concrete expressions in history no longer rule on earth, giving place to the reign of the Lamb, is salvation accomplished. What is essential in Christian theology is not the expectation of salvation of the world but its completion with the final elimination of evil. There is no dilemma, therefore, between the present world and the world of the future, which has so often led to dread, despair and resignation.

4. Christ is the "first-born of all creation" (Col. 1:15); "in him all things... were created" (v.16); "in him all things hold together" (v.17); but he is also "the first-born from the dead" (v.18); and through him God reconciled "all things, whether on earth or in heaven" (v.20). What makes this passage unique for its soteriological significance is unquestionably the use of the word *panta* (all things), a word that occurs no less than eight times(!) in the christological hymn proper (Col. 1:15-20). Christ has wrought salvation not only for all humankind but also for the entire cosmos, the whole creation. Here the emphasis is not just on God's immanence but on the cosmic effect of God's power working in Christ and his body the church.

There was a prevalent Jewish belief that after the fall the entire cosmos, human beings and nature alike, fell into a state of alienation – in human beings by reason of sin, and in all creation by the loss of unity, harmony and beauty. As a result, God's creation fell into the captivity of intermediary (angelic) powers. Christ redeemed the world and took away the control these angelic powers exercised upon humanity. According to various New Testament texts (most notably Rom. 8:20-23), this redemption is not limited to liberation of individuals from sin, death and the satanic powers but is extended even to liberation from alienation, oppression and injustice. It goes even beyond, however, being expected to cover the restoration of the whole creation. The uniqueness of the Colossians passage lies in the fact that this state of cosmic restoration to its original harmony is already a present reality. And according to the neglected Marcan passage (Mark 16:15), this truth is the primary object in Christian mission and evangelism, for the disciples of Christ are sent to proclaim the good news to the entire creation (*pasēi tēi ktīsei*).

This doctrine is nowhere better presented than in Orthodox iconography. Icons in the original Byzantine art do not express a de-materialization of the depicted scenery, as was wrongly believed in the past. What they actually express is the reverse process, i.e. the transfiguration, and consequently sanctification, of matter. It is not only the holy figures that are treated with this transfigural technique but nature too. The material and cosmic elements that surround the holy figures are also transformed and flooded by grace. The icon reveals how the entire creation, humans and nature alike, can and will be transformed into the harmony and beauty that they originally possessed before the fall, but also into that which they will acquire to a much greater extent at the eschaton. It was firmly believed that not just humankind but the cosmos in its entirety participates in God's redemption in Christ. The same conviction lies behind the fundamental Orthodox teaching of *theosis*, for the notion of deification, far from implying disregard of matter, mainly refers to the body's redemption and the restoration to the glory that the whole creation possessed before the fall but will also acquire in its fullness at the eschaton.

IV

There has been an endless debate in the history of our Christian theology as to the relationship in terms of priority between faith and love, between dogma and ethics, between *orthodoxia* and *orthopraxia*, even between faith and order on the one hand, and mission and evangelism, on the other. It is very often argued that love (praxis) comes only as a consequence of faith (theory), or that the former is the ultimate virtue, the achievement of which presupposes all the other virtues, including faith (St John of the Ladder). There is much truth in the argument, however, that Christian theology would never have reached its climax – i.e.

the final articulation of the trinitarian dogma – had a communal life full of love been fully practised in the early church. "See how these Christians love one another", an ancient Christian apologist pointed out; and St John Chrysostom insisted that church members' behaviour and their mutual love was the only effective missionary method.

If, however, we make the supreme axiomatic definition of our trinitarian theology our starting point, we never enter into the vicious circle of the above dilemmas, and we never fall into the trap of such tragic and schizophrenic dichotomy. All fundamental Christian dogmas are conceived as the inevitable consequence of the inner communion and love of the Holy Trinity. There can be no other expression of faith than communion and love. This is perfectly demonstrated in the Johannine passage:

> I give you a new commandment, that you love one another. Just as I have loved you, you also should love one another. By this everyone will know that you are my disciples, if you have love for one another. (John 13:34-35)

I will very briefly comment on how this trinitarian love was understood in our past (apostolic and post-apostolic) and present (ecumenical) history and has been projected (1) in our self-understanding (ecclesiology), (2) in our evangelistic witness (missiology), and (3) in our social but at the same time cosmic responsibility (socio-cosmology).

1. By nature, the church cannot reflect the worldly image of a secular organization, which is normally based on power and domination. Rather, it embraces the kenotic image of the Holy Trinity, which is based on love and communion. This image is nowhere expressed better than in the self-understanding of the early (apostolic and post-apostolic) church.

Using many different terms, the early Christian community viewed itself as a true expression and continuation of the Old Testament people of God. It was not so much a religious organization as a people whom God had called. The consciousness that when God created a new community he created a *people* distinguished the Christian church from the guilds, clubs and religious societies so typical of the Greco-Roman period. It is quite significant that the first Christian community used for itself the term *ekklēsia* in its Old Testament meaning of assembly or community.

Similarly, St Paul builds upon this charismatic notion of the church by his teaching that the church is the *sōma Christou* (body of Christ), thus tying it into the semitic concept of corporate personality. In this body, individual members exercise a variety of charismata for the building up of the body, all under the oversight and authority of Christ, its only head and authority.[27]

The Johannine figure of the vine (John 15:1-8) is equally impressive. As with the Pauline term *sōma*, the double scheme *ampelos-klēmata* (vine-branches) indicates the special relationship existing between Christ and people, which reveals the inner basis of ecclesial life. The other New Testament figures for the church – "household of faith" (Eph. 2:11-21), "fellowship" (1 Cor. 1:9 etc), "bride of Christ" (Eph. 1:31-32; Rev. 21:9), "little flock" (Luke 12:32 etc.), "family of God" (1 Pet. 4:17) etc. – all point in the same direction: namely that the new community is a *people* bound together by love and the Spirit provided by God in Christ, and not by external structure.

From Jesus of Nazareth and the apostles to Ignatius, the early teaching about the nature of the church consistently stressed its eschatological nature, not issues of hierarchy or of authority. From the outset, the early Christian community thus viewed itself as manifesting the kingdom of God on earth, an emphasis the early great theologians consistently maintained.

The ecclesiological problem, therefore, for our churches, which is so important an issue in our ecumenical discussions, is a matter not so much of organization and structure but of eschatological orientation. And there is no better way to rediscover our eschatological self-consciousness than through the eucharist as the sacrament of love, communion, sacrifice and sharing.[28]

2. All churches within the ecumenical movement have eventually realized, following the kenotic example of Christ, that love in fact means that they leave for a while their selfish theological preoccupations and proceed to a "common" evangelistic witness.[29] They have realized that, according to the Matthaean discourse of our Lord on the last judgment (Matt. 25:31-46), what really matters is not so much accepting, and believing in, the abundant love of our triune God (confessional, religious exclusiveness) but exemplifying it to the world through witness (ecclesial inclusiveness). What will prompt churches to embrace such a difficult task? It will not be merely because they are conscious of their share of responsibility, no matter to what extent, for the scandalous division of the one body of Christ and for that reason feel the burden of contributing to the work of the Holy Spirit for the restoration of the broken unity of the church lying on their shoulders; or because common witness is the only visible sign that gives credibility to the church in the eyes of the outside world, until the blessed moment comes when we all, around the same eucharistic table of church unity, share the same eucharistic cup and bread; or even because only in this way can our churches overcome

the temptation of exercising among themselves proselytism – that terrible caricature of evangelism, a kind of counterwitness – and rediscover the catholicity of the church.[30] Rather, churches will act when they realize that the ultimate goal and the raison d'être of the church go far beyond denominational boundaries, beyond Christian limitations, even beyond the religious sphere in the conventional sense: it is the manifestation of the kingdom of God, the restoration of God's "household" (*oikos*) in its majestic eschatological splendour;[31] in other words the projection of the inner dynamics (love, communion, sharing etc.) of the Holy Trinity into the world and cosmic realities.

3. Quite a number of theologians have argued that in St Paul's epistles the importance of *faith* for salvation is stressed, whereas in the Johannine writings it is mainly *love* that is constantly emphasized as the sine qua non of Christian life. The great majority of academic theologians, especially since the time of the Reformation, regardless of their denominational tradition, have examined St Paul's theology exclusively on the grounds of the old *sola fide* justification theory. This theory, significant as it is, has in effect pushed into the background the incarnational/socio-cosmic aspects of his teaching. As a result, this great thinker and father of Christian theology has been accused from various quarters of de-radicalizing the words of the historical Jesus and/or of the kerygma of the early church.

I will focus here only on St Paul's collection project, the most representative side of his multifarious missionary praxis, which can serve as a test case showing how unjust the above accusation is. The project occupied a much greater part in the early church's activity than that presupposed in Acts, for St Paul's entire third missionary trip was almost exclusively devoted to the transfer of the collection to the Jerusalem mother church. Whatever the origin (half-shekel, temple tax?) or its connections (Antiochean collection in Acts 11:27-30, 12:25?), it was St Paul who attached special theological significance to the collection project. Beyond its ecumenical, ecclesiological and eschatological characteristic, its ultimate goal, according to St Paul's thinking – mainly presented in 2 Corinthians 8-9 – was the ideal of *equal distribution and communion of material wealth.* Using a wide variety of terms to describe the collection project (*charis, koinōnia, diakonia, leitourgia, eucharistia* etc.), St Paul understood the collection as the social response of the body of Christ to God's will. For him, and the rest of the Christian community, this act was not simply a social-ethical one but the inevitable response to the kingdom of God inaugurated in Christ.[32]

V

In the light of all the above, I would like to end with some practical remarks and recommendations:

1. The thorny issue of proselytism can be solved only with a profound theological reconsideration of the notion of Christian mission combined with ecclesiology and social ethics,[33] with the involvement and active participation also of non-WCC-member groups. Gospel, evangelism, mission are not for inner consumption of the church. They are primarily aimed at the world. Theology in the church has always tried to have a common language with the world in order to explain the gospel in terms of a given culture. The problem in today's "post-Christian era" stems from the fact that there is no more common language with the outside world.

2. The reasons for not solving the problem of proselytism within the ecumenical movement after so many efforts and joint statements are to be traced in some inherent unresolved problems in the ecumenical movement. One is the Toronto statement (1950) with its neutral ecclesiology, which allows every member church to have its own basic beliefs (and for some Protestant groups, a universal proselytizing mission constitutes the core of their doctrine).[34] A second problem is that proselytism is always related to – in fact is the inevitable consequence of – "religious liberty". Such liberty is a by-product of the Western ideal of human rights and above all of individualism, which is incompatible with koinonia, the heart of Eastern Orthodoxy.[35]

3. To be consistent with its outright condemnation of proselytism, Orthodoxy should abandon also any kind of similar activities in the West. There used to be a fine ethos, which is now fading away, not to consecrate for the diaspora Orthodox communities any bishop to a place belonging to the West, thus respecting the jurisdiction of the church of Rome, and consequently of Western Christianity, of the ancient, undivided, holy, catholic church.[36]

NOTES

[1] Cf. my "Unity and Ecumenicity: The Cosmic and Social Dimension of Orthodoxy (A Comment on the Message of the Primates of the Orthodox Churches)" (in Greek), in *Lex Orandi: Studies of Liturgical Theology*, Ekklesia-Koinonia-Oikoumene 9, Thessaloniki, 1994, pp.157-66, originally published in *Kath' Odon* 2 (1992), pp.119-25. In my comment, despite a generally positive appraisal, I made a few critical remarks regarding Orthodoxy's understanding of mission and proselytism (pp.160-61).

[2] I do not wish to discard the historical or exegetical-critical approaches; on the contrary, I build upon them. I propose to tackle the issue from a biblical angle, mainly because that is my academic speciality.

3 For a thorough examination of the issue from the Orthodox side, see an article by the metropolitan of Ephesus, C. Konstantinidis, "Proselytism, the Ecumenical Movement and the Orthodox Church" (in Greek), in *Orthodoxoi Katopseis*, vol. 4, Katerini, 1991, pp.45-134; see also Leon Zander, "Ecumenism and Proselytism," *International Review of Missions*, 3, 1951, pp.259ff.

4 See a recent paper circulated by G. Lemopoulos entitled "Threats and Hopes for Our Ecumenical Credibility: An Orthodox Reflection on 'Proselytism' and 'Common Witness'", with a substantial number of references and bibliography.

5 Cf. the most important documents and books on the issue, such as *Common Witness: A Joint Document of the Working Group of the Roman Catholic Church and the WCC*, WCC Mission Series, Geneva, 1982; the document *Towards Common Witness: A Call to Adopt Responsible Relationships in Mission and to Renounce Proselytism, Geneva, 1998*; and I. Bria, ed., *Martyria-Mission*, Geneva, 1980. Even *Mission and Evangelism: An Ecumenical Affirmation*, Geneva, 1982, WCC Mission Series 1985, is an attempt to correctly interpret the classical missionary terminology. Cf. also the most recent agreed statement of the Dorfweil, Germany, consultation of KEK with the European Baptist Federation and the European Lausanne Committee for World Evangelization (12-13 June 1995), "Aspects of Mission and Evangelization in Europe Today".

6 Cf. the tension in the recent history of the world Christian mission, which resulted in the tragic separation and the eventual formation of the Lausanne Movement for World Evangelization.

7 M. Goodman, *Mission and Conversion: Proselytizing in the Religious History of the Roman Empire*, Oxford, 1994, p.3.

8 *Ibid.*

9 *Ibid.*, p.4.

10 *Ibid.*

11 *Ibid.*, p.7.

12 Quite recently D.J. Bosch (*Transforming Mission: Paradigm Shifts in Theology of Mission*, New York, 1991) has used a "paradigm-shift theory" to describe the development of Christian understanding of mission down to the most recent ecumenical era.

13 On the recent history of Christian mission, see J. Verkuyl, *Contemporary Missiology: An Introduction* (Eng. trans.), Grand Rapids, Mich., 1978.

14 K. Raiser, *Ecumenism in Transition: A Paradigm Shift in the Ecumenical Movement*, Geneva, 1991 (translated with modifications from the German original *Ökumene im Übergang*, Munich, 1989), p.34.

15 *Ibid.*, pp.79ff.

16 For an early survey by an Orthodox, see one by the archbishop of Albania, Anastasios Yannoulatos, *Various Christian Approaches to the Other Religions: A Historical Outline*, Athens, 1971.

17 This comes from the famous passage in Acts 4:12: "There is salvation in no one else, for there is no other name under heaven given among mortals by which we must be saved."

18 For the relation of mission to dialogue, as well as the repeatedly expressed concern over "syncretism", see K. Raiser, *Ecumenism in Transition*, pp.55ff.; see also the partisan work from the "old paradigm" by W.A. Visser 't Hooft, *No Other Name: The Choice between Syncretism and Christian Universalism*, London, 1963.

19 Cf. the work by the metropolitan of Pergamon, John Zizioulas, *Being as Communion*, New York, 1985.

20 Cf. A.I.C. Heron, ed., *The Forgotten Trinity*, London, 1991.

21 Cf. Metropolitan George Khodre, "Christianity in a Pluralistic World: The Economy of the Holy Spirit", *The Ecumenical Review*, 23, 1971, pp.118-28.

22 Cf. Thomas F. Best and Günther Gassmann, eds, *On the Way to Fuller Koinonia: Official Report of the Fifth World Conference on Faith and Order*, Geneva, 1994, pp.256-57. See also C.M. Robeck Jr's paper "Evangelization, Proselytizing and Common Witness: A Pentecostal Perspective"(unpublished manuscript), p.5.

23 I. Bria, ed., *Go Forth in Peace*, WCC Mission Series, Geneva, 1986, p.3.

24 Cf. N. Nissiotis, "The Witness and the Service of the Eastern Orthodoxy to the One Undivided Church", *The Ecumenical Review*, 14, 1962, pp.192-202; also in C. Patelos, ed., *The Orthodox Church in the Ecumenical Movement*, Geneva, 1978, pp.231-41. This article was Nissiotis' keynote address to the third WCC assembly at New Delhi in 1961.

25 Cf. St Chrysostom's comment on this petition, quoted at the end of ch. 6 below.

26 K. Raiser, *Ecumenism in Transition*, pp.102ff.

[27] For further detail concerning the early Christian terminology and teaching regarding the church, cf. 5 below.

[28] More on this in ch. 5 in this volume.

[29] Cf. among other important contributions L. Newbigin, "Common Witness and Unity", *International Review of Mission*, 69, 1980, pp.160ff.

[30] G. Lemopoulos rightly suggests that it is now time to move beyond the idea of "common witness" and explore the need for a "common mission" ("Threats and Hopes", p.14). This idea presupposes the above eucharistic and trinitarian analysis, and not a return to a christocentric universalism, which would be an undesired return to the "old mission paradigm". It also, however, requires a "common ecclesiology", which is still a desideratum.

[31] Raiser, *Ecumenism in Transition*, pp.102ff.

[32] It is time, I think, for our churches to revive this very significant project, which in today's ecclesiastical practice (both Eastern and Western) has degenerated into an underemphasized institution, without the social and ecumenical dimensions St Paul gave it. This is perhaps a more authentic evangelistic act than the old-fashioned universal proselytizing mission, especially in the narrow confessional perspective.

[33] Cf. Best and Gassmann, *On the Way to Fuller Koinonia*, as well as the WCC publication *Costly Unity*, Geneva, 1992.

[34] Cf. "The Toronto Statement", *The Ecumenical Review*, 13, 1960, pp.85ff.

[35] More on this in J. Zizioulas, "Communion and Otherness", *St Vladimir's Theological Quarterly*, 34, 1994, pp.347-61. Cf. however, a more positive evaluation from an Orthodox perspective in Kostas Delikostantis, *Human Rights: A Western Ideology or an Ecumenical Ethos?* (in Greek), Thessaloniki, 1995.

[36] This study was dedicated to Dr Anastasios Yannoulatos, archbishop of Tirana and all Albania, an active member of the ecumenical movement, and for a number of years moderator of the Commission on World Mission and Evangelism, on the occasion of his 40 years of active missionary activity. Yannoulatos is the theologian and ecclesiastical figure who more than any other in the Orthodox world has contributed to the field of Christian mission. He not only devoted his entire life to Christian witness, the most important but at the same time most neglected area in the Orthodox church; he was also the pioneer in the academic discipline of Orthodox missiology. One could fairly say that he has been the scholar who practically single-handedly introduced the course to the curricula of the Orthodox theological schools and seminaries.

4. The Eucharistic Perspective
of the Church's Mission

It is indeed a great honour and a privilege for me to be invited to address this major inter-Orthodox theological gathering on the very significant and also very challenging topic: "The mission of the church today and tomorrow". Significant, because it concentrates on the most important aspect of the church's life (one somehow neglected in our tradition): its mission; but also challenging, because – contrary to our recent practice – the focus is not on the past, on our invaluable and most precious tradition, but on the future.[1]

If one can sum up the major developments of the past three conferences, one would note the missionary concern to adjust our legacy with the present reality, the main focus being ecclesiology and its consequences, i.e. the new ecumenical reality. Indeed, this present congress finds our church – and our theology as the prophetic conscience of the church – at the threshold of a new, unprecedented and very challenging situation, amidst a fast-moving world, one marked by divisions, growing social inequality, serious ecological crisis, and above all by the still-persisting, scandalous disunity among Christians who confess, and believe in, *our triune God*; in the *one body of Christ*, our only hope (1 Tim. 1:1); and in the *communion of the Holy Spirit*, who constitutes the whole institution of the church and "has called all in unity".[2] Such a world desperately needs our authentic Orthodox *martyria* (witness).

I

The trinitarian approach seems to be the prevailing one among almost all Orthodox in recent times.[3] The preparatory committee's sug-

● This chapter is adapted from the author's keynote address at the fourth conference of Orthodox theological schools, Bucharest, 11-17 August 1996, a transcription of which will appear in the proceedings of that conference. An earlier version appeared in the *Scholarly Annual of the Theological School of the University of Thessaloniki*, n.s., 7, 1997, pp. 19-44, and is reprinted here by permission of the publisher.

gestion, therefore, that the main papers should have trinitarian theology as a starting point is absolutely legitimate. Without undermining this suggestion, and although the trinitarian approach is widely recognized and applied more and more, even by non-Orthodox in dealing with current theological issues,[4] I have decided to approach the main theme of the conference from the *eucharistic* perspective. I came to this decision not so much in order to avoid a strictly contextual approach;[5] rather, for purely methodological reasons I consider it not only as much more appropriate for us Orthodox, but also as more logical.[6]

It is time, I think, to distance ourselves as much as possible from the syndrome prevalent in modern scholarship of making texts dominant over experience, theology over ecclesiology. Many scholars cling to the dogma, imposed by the post-Enlightenment and post-Reformation hegemony over all scholarly theological outlook (and not only in the field of biblical scholarship or of Western and, in particular, Protestant theology), which can be summarized as follows: what constitutes the core of our Christian faith, of our Orthodox tradition if you like, can be extracted only from expressed theological views, from a certain *depositum fidei* – be it the Bible, the writings of the fathers, or the canons and certain decisions of the councils. Very rarely, in fact, is there any serious reference to the eucharistic communion event that has been responsible for and produced these views.

It is my firm conviction that out of the three main characteristics of what is generally known as Orthodox theology – namely its eucharistic, trinitarian, and hesychastic dimensions – only the first can bear a universal and ecumenical significance. The last dimension and important feature, our hesychastic tradition,[7] marks a decisive development in Eastern Christian theology and spirituality after the schism between East and West, a development that has determined, together with other factors, the mission of our church in recent history. And the trinitarian dimension constitutes the highest expression of Christian theology ever produced by human thought in its attempt to grasp the mystery of God, occurring after Christianity's dynamic encounter with Greek culture.[8] Nevertheless, it was only because of the eucharistic experience, the matrix of all theology and spirituality of our church, that all theological and spiritual climaxes in our church have been actually achieved.

Modern theological scholarship (biblical and liturgical) has virtually proven that the eucharist was "lived" in the early Christian community not as a mystery cult but as a foretaste of the coming kingdom of God, a proleptic manifestation within the tragic realities of history of an authentic life of communion, unity, justice and equality, with no practical differentiation (soteriological or in any other respect) between Jews and Gentiles, slaves and free, men and women (cf. Gal. 3:28). This was, after all, the real meaning of the Johannine phrase "eternal life" and St Ignatius's expression "medicine of immortality". According to some historians, the church was able a few generations later, with the important contribution of the Greek fathers of the golden age, to come up with the doctrine of the Trinity, and much later to further develop the important distinction between substance and energies, only because of the eschatological experience of koinonia by the early Christian community in the eucharist (both vertical with its head, and horizontal among the people of God, and by extension with all humanity), an experience that ever since continues to constitute the only expression of the church's self-consciousness, its mystery par excellence.[9]

II

The Christian understanding of mission undoubtedly must be determined by the teaching, life and work of Christ. His teaching, however, and especially his life and work, cannot be properly understood without reference to the eschatological expectations of Judaism. Without entering the complexities of Jewish eschatology, we could say very briefly that it was interwoven with the expectation of the coming of the Messiah. In the "last days" of history (the eschaton), he would establish his kingdom by calling the dispersed and afflicted people of God into one place to become one body united around him. The statement in John 11:51-52 about the Messiah's role is extremely important. There the writer interprets the words of the Jewish high priest by affirming that "he prophesied that Jesus was about to die... not for the nation only, but to *gather into one* the dispersed children of God".[10]

Throughout the gospels Christ identifies himself with this Messiah. We see this in the various messianic titles he chose for himself, or at least as witnessed by the most primitive Christian tradition ("Son of man", "Son of God" etc., most of which had a collective meaning, whence the Christology of "corporate personality"). We see it as well in the parables of the kingdom, which summarize his teaching, proclaiming that his coming initiates the new world of the kingdom of God, in the Lord's prayer, but also in his conscious acts (e.g. the selection of the Twelve). In short, Christ identified himself with the Messiah of the eschaton who would be the centre of the gathering of the dispersed people of God.

The early church developed its ecclesiology, and in turn its mission-ary practice, on this radical eschatological teaching of the historical Jesus about the kingdom of God (which, as modern biblical research has shown, moves dialectically between the "already" and the "not yet"; in other words, it has begun already in the present but will be completed in its final authentic form in the eschaton). From the writings of Paul, John and Luke, in addition to other works, we see this teaching reflected in images of the church as the body of Christ, as vine, and especially as unity. The apostle Paul in particular was absolutely convinced that all who have believed in Christ have been incorporated into his body through baptism, completing with the eucharist their incorporation into the one people of God. The fourth gospel develops this radical eschato-logical teaching even further in regard to the unity of the people of God around Christ and their incorporation into Christ's body – above all, through the eucharist.

The main contribution primitive Christian theology made to the development of this messianic eschatology was the common belief of almost all theologians of the early church, emphasized and underlined most sharply by St Luke, that with Christ's resurrection and especially with Pentecost, the eschaton had already entered history and that the messianic eschatological community becomes a reality each time the church, the new Israel, the dispersed people of God, gathers *epi to auto* (in one place), especially when it gathers to celebrate the holy eucharist. This development is undoubtedly the starting point of Christian mission, the springboard of the church's witnessing exodus to the world, which in fact interpreted the imminent expectation of the parousia in a dynamic and radical way.

The missiological imperatives of the early church stem exactly from this awareness of the church as an eschatological, dynamic, radical, and corporate reality, commissioned to witness the kingdom of God "on earth as it is in heaven" (Matt. 6:10 par).[11] The apostles were commis-sioned to proclaim not a set of given religious convictions, doctrines, moral commands etc. but the coming kingdom, the good news of a new eschatological reality that had as its centre the crucified and resurrected Christ, the incarnation of God the Logos and his dwelling among us human beings, and his continuous presence through the Holy Spirit, in a life of communion, experienced in their "eucharistic" (in the wider sense) life. That is why they are called holy – because they belonged to that chosen race of the people of God. That is why they were considered "royal priesthood" – because all of them, without exception (not just some special caste, such as the priests or Levites), have priestly and spiritual authority to practise in the diaspora the work of the priestly class, and are reminded at the same time to be worthy of their election through their exemplary life and works.[12] That is why they were called to walk towards unity ("that they may become completely one", John 17:23), to abandon all deeds of darkness.

III

No doubt this initial, horizontal historical eschatology – which identifies the church not by what it is in the present but by what it will become in the eschaton, and at the same time suggests that the church's mission is the dynamic journey of the people of God as a whole towards the eschaton, with the eucharist as the point of departure – became interwoven from the very first days of the church's life with a vertical one, which put the emphasis on a more personal understanding of salvation. No matter for what reasons,[13] from the time of St Paul there has been a shift of the centre of gravity from the (eucharistic) experience to the (Christian) message, from eschatology to Christology (and further and consequently to soteriology), from the event (the kingdom of God), to the bearer and centre of this event (Christ, and more precisely his sacrifice on the cross).[14] The eucharist (the *theia koinōnia*, divine communion), however, always remained the sole expression of the church's identity.

Although some theologians consider this second concept, which was mingled with the original biblical/semitic thought, as stemming from Greek philosophers (Stoics and others), nevertheless it is more than clear that the horizontal-eschatological view was the predominant one in the New Testament and in other early Christian writings. The vertical-soteriological view was always understood within the context of the horizontal-eschatological perspective as supplemental and complementary. This is why the liturgical experience of the early church is incomprehensible without its social dimension (see Acts 2:42-47, 1 Corinthians 11; Heb. 13:10-16; Justin, *1 Apol.* 67; Irenaeus, *Adver. Her.* 18:1, etc.).

This missiological perspective and experience in the early church is also clearly reflected within its liturgical order, which from the time of St Ignatius of Antioch onwards considers the eschatological people of God, gathered in one place around Christ, as reflected in the offices of the church: the bishop is "in the place and as image of Christ", while the presbyters around him represent the apostles. Above all, it is the eucharistic gathering that authentically expresses the mystery of the church. Here, in the gathering of the community around the bishop, the community does not propagate its faith on the basis of a sacramental redemption from worldly suffering, nor does it proclaim personal perfection and individual salvation (though neither are these necessarily excluded); rather, it witnesses to its nature as the proleptic manifestation of the eschatological kingdom of God.[15]

This eucharistic/liturgical understanding of the early Christian community's identity, considering the church as an icon of the eschaton, also resulted in an understanding of its mission as an imperative duty to witness its being as an authentic expression in a particular time and place of the eschatological glory of the kingdom of God, with all that this could imply for social life. It is to be noted that a conviction began to grow among church writers, beginning with the author of Hebrews (10:1) and more fully developed in the writings of St Maximus the Confessor, that the events of the Old Testament were a *skia* (shadow) of future riches, and that present church reality is only an *ikōn* (image) of the *alētheia* (truth), which is only to be revealed in the eschaton.

IV

This fundamental biblical and early Christian understanding of mission, based on the eucharistic/liturgical and eschatological understanding of the church, by the third century AD began gradually to fall out of favour (under the intense ideological pressure of Christian Gnosticism and especially Platonism), or at best to coexist with concepts promulgated by the catechetical school of Alexandria. The type of spirituality and Christian witness that developed around these circles did not have the eschaton (the Ω, omega) as its point of reference. Rather, it focused on the creation (the A, alpha), the *archē* (beginnings) of human beings, humanity's primal state of blessedness in paradise before the fall. The main representatives of this school, Clement of Alexandria and Origen, gave Christian ecclesiology, and by extension its missiology, a new direction that, as Metropolitan John Zizioulas emphatically put it, was "not merely a change, but a complete reversal".[16] Thus the church ceases to be an icon of the eschaton; it becomes instead an icon of the origin of beings, of creation,[17] with Christ being considered primarily as the source of humankind's union with God and as the recapitulation, in some sense, of human fallen nature. But if "recapitulation" was understood biblically earlier in the church's life,[18] with the Alexandrians the concept is torn completely from its biblical roots in eschatology. The eschaton is no longer the focal point and apex of the divine economy. The direction of interest has been reversed, and now the focus is on creation. Thus we have a cosmological approach to the church and to its mission, not a historical one, as in the holy scriptures. The church is now understood, completely apart from the historical community, as a perfect and eternal idea. Naturally, therefore, interest in mission and the historical process has diminished, together with interest in the institutional reality of the church, whose purpose is now characterized, at best, as a sanatorium of souls. The church's mission is now directed not in bringing about synergically and proleptically the kingdom of God, but towards the salvation of the souls of every individual Christian. Historically this new development in the church's missiological attitude is connected with the origins of monasticism.[19] Without ignoring the communal and eschatological character of authentic Orthodox monasticism,[20] the fact remains that the central core of Alexandrian theology, with which monasticism was historically connected, was a departure from the initial radical and dynamic horizontal eschatology of the New Testament and of the early post-apostolic Christian tradition – in some cases even in direct opposition to it.

The consequences for Christian spirituality, and more particularly for mission, of this theology and ecclesiology were immense. The church's common worship, its offices and its institutions lost virtually all meaning as icons of the eschaton.[21] Under this peculiar mysticism, salvation is no longer connected to the coming kingdom, to the anticipation of a new eschatological community with a more authentic structure. Now salvation is identified with the soul's union with the Logos and therefore with the *catharsis*, the purification, from all that prohibits union with the primal Logos, including all that is material, tangible, historical. The *maranatha* of the Pauline communities and the *erchou kyrie* (come, Lord!) of the seer/prophet of the Apocalypse are replaced by continuous prayer and the struggle against the demons and the flesh.

In contrast, therefore, to the eucharistic/liturgical understanding of the Christian witness, this therapeutic/cathartic view puts the emphasis on the effort towards purification of the soul from passions, and towards healing of the fallen nature of human beings. In other words, the reference point is not the eschatological glory of the kingdom of God but the state of blessedness in paradise before the fall. Naturally, then, the church's mission can hardly be seen in terms of kingdom theology, but in terms of individual salvation.[22]

V

These two basic understandings of ecclesiology, spirituality and mission remained as parallel forces, sometimes meeting together and forming a creative unity, and other times moving apart and creating dilemmas and conflicts. Where should one search for the starting point of the church's mission to the world and in fact to the entire cosmos? Where can one find personal wholeness and salvation? In the eucharistic gathering around the bishop, where one could overcome creatively all social polarities and schizophrenic dichotomies (spirit/matter, transcendence/immanence, coming together/going forth etc.)? Or in the desert, the hermitage, the monastery, where presumably the effort of catharsis and healing of passions through ascetic discipline of the individual is more effective? This was, and remains, a critical dilemma in the life of the church, especially in the East.

Without any doubt the centre of the church's mission and spirituality, with few exceptions, has always remained the eucharist, the sole place where the church becomes what it actually is: the people of *God*, the body of *Christ*, the communion of the *Holy Spirit* – a glimpse and a foretaste of the coming kingdom of God. However, the crucial question is how to understand this unique sacrament (not just one among many) and mystery of the church.[23] A decisive turning point in this respect came when the high theology of the *corpus areopagiticus* affected our Christian liturgy. Pseudo-Dionysius was undoubtedly the catalyst in the development of the church's liturgy and mission. His theological analyses and reflections made a tremendous impact not only on the shaping of subsequent theology and monastic spirituality but also on the very heart of biblical radical eschatology, as expressed in the eucharistic liturgy,[24] with significant consequences for the church's mission.[25]

From the mid-Byzantine period onward[26] the original understanding of eucharist as a springboard for mission, as the mystery par excellence of the church, as a feast of eschatological joy,[27] as a gathering *epi to auto* of the eschatological people of God,[28] as an authentic expression of fellowship among people, and as participation in the word and the supper of the Lord[29] is no longer prominent. Once a realistic expression of the body of Christ and a communion of the Holy Spirit, it now became a place of theophany, a sign and point of meeting with the mystery of the divine. Active participation in the divine liturgy no longer means participation in the processions, in the singing, in listening and understanding of the readings and the sermons, not even in receiving communion. Now the main point of all liturgical life is the uplifting of the individual believers, their transfer through faith from *history* to *theōria*, from visible symbols and actions to the transcendent reality that they depict. In this way, little by little, for the great mass of people, but also for the clerical vanguard of the church, including most theologians, the eucharist, the church's *leitourgia* (the people's work), lost its fundamental ecclesial dimension, and with it all its missionary significance and power.[30]

It is a real wonder how the four main processional sections of our Eastern liturgy survived into the present, even with many deviations along the way.[31] Thus (1) the solemn entrance of the whole worshiping community into the church building was reduced to the *Little Entrance* with the gospel, without the people's participation. The laos simply view the performance. (2) The same thing happens with the *Great Entrance*: No longer do the people participate directly in offering the gifts of creation, with the one presiding over the community "referring" them back (anaphora) to the Creator. Instead, the people now "offer" the gifts as "prosphora" (liturgical bread) outside the eucharistic liturgy during the *proskomide*, a rite that derives from this period and that was transferred as a preparation of the holy gifts before the eucharistic liturgy proper. (3) The *kiss of peace* ("let us love one another"), a dynamic act of community reconciliation and therefore the sole precondition for participation in true worship (Matt. 5:23-26), is limited now exclusively to the clergy. Finally, (4) the *communion*, the culminating and most important act of the eucharistic rite, is shifted and completely transformed from a corporate act that anticipates the eschatological kingdom into an act of individual piety. What is even more tragic, however, is that the participation of the entire people in the sacrament of the church (i.e. in receiving communion) was completely abandoned. But without catholic communion, the divine liturgy becomes at best a symbolic reality for spiritual contemplation, and at worst a sterile ritualism.

VI

Having thus far emphasized the significance of the reinforcement of the eucharistic criterion in determining our church's witness, it has become clear that the basic presuppositions of today's mission of the church should necessarily start from the very heart of our (Orthodox) Christian identity: the eucharist, as the only expression of the *being* of the church. All other missiological imperatives are bound to be incomplete and ineffective – not to mention question-begging – as long as the very being of the church in its ontological and fullest expression remains far from a living expression of unity, communion, equality, fellowship, sharing and self-sacrifice; as long as our eucharistic gatherings retain exclusively the status of a sacra-mentalistic (quasi-magic) cultic act, and not proleptic manifestations of the kingdom of God, the only means by which humanity can hope to transcend corruptibility, disintegration, disunity and mortality of the historical reality.

Unfortunately, because of a centuries-long lack of a healthy theolog-ical concern (equal to that of the great fathers of our church), the present sacramental reality of the church was considered as almost unchange-able, with a tragic effect on its authentic witness. The late Fr A. Schme-mann was instrumental during his lifetime in implementing a liturgical renewal in our Orthodox church. He insisted, though, only on the neces-sity of a theological interpretation of our liturgical tradition, thus stop-ping short of a radical rediscovery and reinforcement of the authentic liturgical/eucharistic identity of our church's witness.[32]

In order that a renewal in Christian witness can take place in our Orthodox church, it is necessary as a basic presupposition to turn our attention first to its eucharistic expression, the heart and centre of its ontological identity. I will very briefly refer to the those readjustments (not reforms) in our eucharistic liturgical praxis, that have already taken place as the least steps in our local eucharistic communities, in an effort to regain their authentic "Orthodox" outlook.[33] Only if these steps gain wider acceptance within all autocephalic churches, especially the metro-politan "mother" Orthodox churches, can one hope that the Orthodox witness to a crying world can be both "orthodox" and effective. The most significant of these steps are:[34]

1. The restoration of the *catholic* participation in the eschatological table of the kingdom. This means reception of communion by *all* (not just frequent communion), with no juridical or legalistic preconditions (such as worthiness or strict preparation of the individual faithful),[35] i.e. without any subordination of the sacrament par excellence of the church to other sacraments (repentance, priesthood etc.,[36] which are certainly of lesser importance from the point of view of Orthodox theology).[37]

2. Return to the early Christian status of full and inclusive *participa-tion* of the entire people of God (special/ordained and general/lay priest-

hood, men and women) in the actions, processions and singing of the people),[38] and if possible rehabilitation of the "cathedral office".[39]

3. Step by step replacement of the normal *choir*, (at least of the solitary church singer, the *psaltēs*) by the entire laos (as in the original and authentic Orthodox tradition, according to the demands of all liturgical rubrics). Continue until all these intermediate and merely assisting elements of our liturgical life are done away with – or better, until they become leaders rather than substitutes for the participation of the whole community in the eucharistic drama.

4. Special care that the eucharist, as well as all other liturgical services connected with it (both those of the divine office and the sacramental services, i.e. the holy mysteries), are celebrated in *forms* – symbolic, linguistic, dramatic, etc. – that are profitable to the grassroots faithful and understood by the entire community, the natural co-celebrants of the holy mysteries of the church.[40]

5. Complete abolishment of all the common *prayers read secretly* by the presiding celebrant, especially those of the anaphora in its entirety,[41] as well as those of all other liturgical acts developed later, such as the restriction only to the higher priestly orders of the kiss of love ("let us love one another").

6. Return to the original form of Orthodox *church buildings*, emphasizing all the elements that characterize the pioneering and revolutionary Byzantine architectural techniques of Hagia Sophia, such as the illumination of space, in contrast to the later dim and dull technical style (a result of later influences that were not always theologically healthy, as pointed out above), which instead of directing the community towards the light and joy of the kingdom, unconsciously contributes to a certain individualization of the salvation-event. Also, we should abolish pews and chairs of all kinds from the nave. These were added later, certainly under Western influence, and transform the worshiping people from active co-celebrants to passive attendants of the liturgical actions.

7. Emphasis on all processional, liturgical and participatory elements of our Orthodox liturgy, starting with the re-establishment of the *ambo* and the transfer around it (i.e. outside the sanctuary) of all related parts of our liturgical praxis. This includes the "sacrament of the word" at the divine liturgy and the non-eucharistic services (vespers, matins etc.), according to our ancient canonical order, which fortunately is preserved even today, but only during the hierarchical services, in which the bishop *chorostateī* (stands by the choir, i.e. by the community). In addition, there must be the return of the *Great Entrance* to its original form, i.e.

with a symbolic participation of the entire community at the transfer of the gifts of creation (represented by the deacons alone, the order inter-mediate between the laypeople and the priesthood proper), so that the presiding celebrant simply receives and does not also himself transfer the offerings of the community (cf. again the traditional order of the eucharistic celebration with a presiding bishop). And the rite of the *proskomidē* must return to its original place, i.e. immediately before the *Great Entrance*.

8. Abolishment of the current structure of the *iconostasis*, a develop-ment that has had the unfortunate effect of further separating the clergy from the rest of the people of God. In my view, it would be extremely beneficial for both pastoral and missionary purposes to return to the architectural status immediately after the triumph of the icons, with the only dividing elements between the sanctuary and the nave being high columns and short *thōrakeia*, on top of which small portable icons will be placed, in the place of the gigantic ones. Finally,

9. Highlighting of the exclusively *eschatological character* of the Sunday eucharist by returning to the order of service "sabbaitic typikon", i.e. attaching the Sunday matins to the vespers. The people would experience the mystery/sacrament of the kingdom, and not as one religious rite among others; the eucharistic gathering would become a glimpse and manifestation of the eighth day.

VII

The above readjustments in our eucharistic services are only the minimum needed for a real and authentic eucharistic renewal in our wit-ness to the world; they cannot solve the problem by themselves. To some these readjustments may even sound like *theologia secunda*, not *theolo-gia prima*. But here we are dealing with the being and the identity of the church, without the authentic expression of which (because of external factors and social dynamics) Christianity may well slip to become an authoritarian and oppressive religious system. Without the prophetic voice of theology, the *leitourgia*, the primary expression of the church, and the eucharist as its centre and climax can easily become at best a useless typolatry. At worst it becomes a sacramentalistic (for some, even demonic) ritual, which, instead of directing the Christian community towards the vision of the coming kingdom, leads it to individualistic and mystical paths. And this is something that eventually distances the members of the community from the "other" (and therefore from God, the real "Other"), leading them to death, to hell.

The problem of the church's witness, i.e. the problem of overcoming the evil in the world, is not basically a moral issue. It is primarily and even exclusively an issue of ecclesial significance. The moral and social responsibility of the church (both as an institution and as individual members), as the primary witnessing acts of the body of Christ, is the logical consequence of its ecclesial self-consciousness. It is therefore only by a massive reaffirmation of the eucharistic identity of the church through a radical *liturgical renewal* that our Orthodox church can bear witness to its fundamental characteristics of unity and catholicity. Only then can we hope that today's exclusivity will naturally give place to the priority of communion with the others. Only then will our church definitely and once for all overcome all kinds of nationalistic and ethnocentric behaviour, the worst heresy of our time. Not only would we promote Orthodox unity, we would also actively contribute to the quest both of the visible unity of the church and of the unity of humankind.

In terms of mission, this will also result in moving towards a *common* evangelistic witness. Beyond the biblical imperative,[42] the eucharistic perspective of mission points far beyond denominational boundaries, beyond Christian limitations, even beyond the religious sphere in the conventional sense, and towards the manifestation of the kingdom of God, the restoration the "household" (*oikos*) of God, in its majestic eschatological splendour.

Through a genuine eucharistic revival one can expect to overcome much more easily the corrupted hierarchical order both in society and in the priestly ecclesiastical order, which is a reflection of the fallen earthly order and not of the kenotic divine one. This will inevitably result in the proper traditional "iconic" understanding of all priestly ministries, but it will also lead to a more authentic "conciliar" status in all sectors of the ecclesiastical life (i.e. participation of the entire laos in the priestly, royal and prophetic ministry of the church) and to a genuine community of men and women.

Finally, a eucharistic revival will also help the church to move away from a certain christocentric universalism and towards a trinitarian understanding of the divine reality and of the church's mission that embraces the entire oikoumene as the one household of life. Especially for mission, this means the abandonment of any effort of proselytism, not only among Christians of other denominations, but even among peoples of other religions. *Martyria/witness* and *dialogue* will then replace,

or at least run parallel to, the old missiological terminology. This development will by no means imply abandoning our fundamental Christian
soteriology. It is rather a radical reinterpretation of Christology through
pneumatology, through the rediscovery of the forgotten trinitarian theology of the undivided church, and above all through eucharistic theology.[43]

NOTES

[1] Nevertheless, this new and very promising development in the theological deliberations of our
Orthodox academic institutions, the first in modern history to take place outside the realm of
Greek Orthodoxy, cannot but somehow take into consideration some of the previous achievements in the series of conferences of the modern Orthodox theological schools. Thus, one cannot ignore that the first congress, held in Athens in 1936, was marked by the historic appeal for
a return to the fathers, not as a move towards the past, but as a liberating reaction to the scholastic inclination of our previous theological endeavours (G. Florovsky, "Patristics and Modern
Theology", in A. Alivizatos, ed., *Procès-verbaux du premier congrès de théologie orthodoxe*,
Athens, 1939, pp.238-42). According to the final communiqué of the second congress, held in
1976, also in Athens "evident to all members... were the importance of... fellowship, the need to
understand one another... a deep interest in ecclesiology, particularly in ecumenical research and
activity" (S. Agouridis, ed., *Procès-verbaux du deuxième congrès de théologie orthodoxe*, 1978,
p.574. Finally, in the third congress, which was held in 1987 in Boston on the premises of the
Greek Orthodox Theological School of the Holy Cross, a very bold but undoubtedly pragmatic
view was openly expressed in the keynote address, when it was stated with bitterness that our
modern Orthodox theology has in fact failed "to open any real dialogue with current theological
thinking and with world ideologies at the level of a commonly accepted vocabulary" (S.
Agouridis, "An Assessment of Theological Issues Today", *Greek Orthodox Theological Review*,
38, 1993, pp.29ff).

[2] From the hymns of Pentecost.

[3] I. Bria, ed., *Go Forth in Peace: Orthodox Perspectives on Mission*, Geneva, 1986, p.3; more in
"Orthodoxy and Ecumenism", ch. 2 above.

[4] K. Raiser's book *Ecumenism in Transition: A Paradigm Shift in the Ecumenical Movement*,
Geneva, 1991 (translated with modifications from the German original, *Ökumene im Übergang*,
1989, and now also in Greek translation) is a perfect example of a well-documented argumentation for the necessity and, in our view also, for the right use of trinitarian theology in modern
scholarship.Cf. also Elizabeth A. Johnson, *She Who Is: The Mystery of God in Feminist Theological Discourse*, New York, 1992, especially ch. 10, "Triune God: Mystery of Revelation",
pp.191ff.

[5] A serious attempt to approach the problem of contextual theology has been undertaken by my faculty (Department of Theology of the Aristotle University of Thessaloniki, Greece), which, jointly
with the Ecumenical Institute of Bossey, organized a theological symposium held on 2-3 October
1992 in Thessaloniki on the theme "Classical and Contextual Theology: The Task of Orthodox
Theology in the Post-Canberra Ecumenical Movement". The papers in Greek translation have
been published in the journal *Kath' Odon*, 4, 1993. My keynote paper in a shortened form
appeared also in *Ökumenische Rundschau*, 41, 1993, pp.452-60; for its original form (in Greek)
see also in my *Lex Orandi: Studies of Liturgical Theology*, Thessaloniki, 1994, pp.139-56.

[6] In approaching any specific issue, like the theme of the present conference (i.e. the church and
its mission today and tomorrow), one should avoid the temptation to ignore the primary experience, i.e. the ecclesia and its eucharistic eschatological experience, the matrix of all theology, or
to use a socio-(cultural-)anthropological description of the wider "social space" that produced
all theological interpretations of this experience. It would be a methodological fallacy, however,
to project later theological interpretations onto this primary eschatological experience.

[7] Cf. M. Begzos, "Orthodox Theology and the Future of Its Past" (in Greek), *Ekklēsiastikos Kērykas*, 3, 1991, p.146.

[8] On this debated issue cf. S. Agouridis, *The Holy Trinity and Us*, 1993; *idem*, "Can the Persons of the Trinity Give Rise to Personalistic Views about Humanity?" *Synaxe*, 33, 1990, pp.67-78; Metr. J. Zizioulas, "The Being of God and the Being of Humanity", *Synaxe*, 37, 1991, pp.11-35.

[9] For similar reason, and with all due respect to the proposed scheme (i.e. the preparatory committee's suggestion to elaborate the theme from the Greek Orthodox perspective, which is absolutely legitimate for practical reasons), I propose not to contribute to the subconsciously existing dividing lines within Orthodoxy and expound a strictly "regional" (i.e. Greek Orthodox) point of view, but rather one that is "theological" and "ecumenically Orthodox" (i.e. critical, and sometimes even self-critical). After all, in my Greek Orthodox constituency for some decades now, the prevailing theological paradigm is being determined by the hesychastic rather than the eucharistic tradition of our church. In other words, I will try to expound what I consider, out of my ecclesial (i.e. liturgical) experience, the mission of the "one, holy, catholic and apostolic church" should be.

[10] Cf. also Isa. 66:18; Matt. 25:32; Rom. 12:16; Didache 9:4b; Mart. Pol. 22:3b; 1 Clem. 12:6 etc.

[11] Cf. St Chrysostom's comment on the relevant petition of the Lord's prayer, quoted at the end of ch. 6 below.

[12] J.H. Elliott, *The Elect and the Holy*, 1966, has recovered on the part of the Protestant biblical theology the real meaning of the phrase *basileion hierateuma* (royal priesthood), which has been so vigorously discussed since the time of Luther. Cf. R. Brown, *Priest and Bishop: Biblical Reflections*, 1971.

[13] D. Passakos, in a recent doctoral dissertation under my supervision ("The Eucharist in the Pauline Mission: A Sociological Approach", 1995), analyzed this "paradigm shift" at that crucial moment of early Christianity and claimed that "the eucharist in Paul was understood not only as an icon of the eschata, but also as a missionary event with cosmic and social consequences. The eucharist for him was not only the sacrament of the church but also the sacrament of the world. Within the Pauline communities the eucharist had a double orientation (in contrast to the overall eschatological and other-worldly dimension of it in earlier tradition): towards the world as diastolic movement, and towards God as a systolic movement" (pp.187-88). According to Passakos, "The eucharist for Paul is at the same time an experience of the eschata and a movement towards the eschata" (p.189).

[14] Cf. my *Cross and Salvation* (in Greek), 1983, an English summary of which appears in a paper of mine delivered at the 1984 annual Leuven colloquium ("*Stauros*: Centre of the Pauline Soteriology and Apostolic Ministry", in A. Vanhoye, ed., *L'Apôtre Paul: Personnalité, style et conception du ministère*, Leuven, 1986, pp.246-53).

[15] Cf. Ignatius, *Ad Eph.* 13:1: "Seek, then, to come together more frequently to give thanks and glory to God. For when you gather together frequently, the powers of Satan are destroyed...."

[16] J. Zizioulas, *Issues of Ecclesiology*, Thessaloniki, 1992, p.28.

[17] Under the influence of the ancient Greek philosophy, particularly Platonism, the Alexandrians believed that the original condition of beings represents perfection and that all subsequent history is a decline. The mystery of the incarnation contributes almost nothing to this system of thought. On Origen's soteriology and the minimal salvific significance it gives to the Christ's human nature, see A. Grillmeier, *Christ in Christian Tradition*, Atlanta, 1975; also R. Taft, "The Liturgy of the Great Church: An Initial Synthesis of Structure and Interpretation on the Eve of Iconoclasm", *Dumbarton Oaks Papers*, 34-35, 1980-81, p.62, n. 79.

[18] Cf. St Irenaeus' use of *anakephalaiōsis* (recapitulation) (*Adver. Her.* 3), based on Pauline theology. One can also note how finally St Athanasius the Great articulated this concept more definitively in his classic statement that "He [God] became human so that we could become God" (*On Incarnation*, 54:).

[19] In the Eastern, but also the Western, monasteries, the works of Origen were studied with great reverence, even after his conciliar condemnation (cf. G. Mantzaridis, "Spiritual Life in Palamism", in J. Raitt, B. McGinn and J. Meyendorff, eds, *Christian Spirituality. II: High Middle Ages and Reformation*, 1988, p.216).

[20] At this point it is essential to point out that this general trend should not be confused with the authentic understanding of the Christian theology of monasticism. It would be a serious mistake not to refer to the various corrective theological interventions through which the monastic movement was incorporated into the life of the church (including the cenobitic system of Pachomius, the

Vita Antoniae by Athanasius the Great, the communal and ecclesiological orientation of monasticism by Basil the Great, the eschatological meaning given to therapeutic ecclesiology and "the bold synthesis of all previous theological experience" by the monk Maximus the Confessor). One should not ignore the various theological approaches that stress the eschatological dimension of Eastern monasticism, which characterize it as a sign of the kingdom and a life of repentance. The latter is clearly an eschatological concept based on Christ's words in his very first proclamation: "The kingdom of God is at hand; repent" (Mark 1:15 par.). The monastic's life is considered an angelic life because, at least according to the interpretation of Pachomius, celibacy was connected to the future kingdom on the basis of the Lord's words: "For in the resurrection they neither marry nor are given in marriage, but are like angels in heaven" (Matt. 22:30), and "there are eunuchs who have made themselves eunuchs for the sake of the kingdom of heaven" (Matt. 19:12 par.).

21 According to W. Jardine Grisbrooke ("The Formative Period – Cathedral and Monastic Offices", in C. Jones, G. Wainwright, E. Yarnold and P. Bradshaw, eds, *The Study of Liturgy*, New York, 1988, 2d ed. 1992, 403-20), monasticism as a lay movement in its initial stages was not only a detachment from, and rejection of, the world; it also believed that priesthood was incompatible with the monastic order (p.404). It is not accidental that during the first stage of the development of Christian monasticism, the monks cut themselves off from common worship to devote themselves to continuous private prayer. The notion of continuous prayer was not new (cf. 1 Thess. 5:17); the novelty was its interpretation. Whereas the early Christians considered that every act or expression could be regarded as prayer, now in some monastic circles private prayer as such in fact replaced everything else, most notably mission (cf. A. Schmemann, *Introduction to Liturgical Theology*, p.160 in the 1991 Greek translation). This defection from the original spirituality of the early church resulted in the creation of new forms and concepts of worship, which we see especially in the formation of what later came to be known as the monastic typikon. Within this important spiritual movement, worship no longer takes its meaning from the eschatological perspective of the eucharist but is designed instead to be used primarily as a tool to carve deeply within the mind of the monastics the principle of continuous individual prayer. As Grisbrooke points out, this "has nothing to do with corporate worship, but is rather a helpful expression of individual private prayer practised in common", p.405.

22 This very fact was completely overlooked in G. Panagopoulos and P. Andriopoulos, "Eucharist and Katharsis Undivided in the Tradition", *Synaxe*, 51, 1994, pp.105-16, which was a response to an abridged version of my article "Eucharistic and Therapeutic Spirituality" in my *Lex Orandi*, pp.107-35, which appeared in *Synaxe*, 49, 1994, 53-72, as "Eucharist or Katharsis the Criterion of Orthodoxy?" I found this response hasty and also arrogant and thus unworthy of a scholarly rebuttal. I believe that the best answer to their views was provided by Metropolitan J. Zizioulas' article in the very same issue (see n. 33 below).

23 In order to have a clear view of the problem, one can compare the eucharistic prayers of the anaphoras (the earliest ones, and particularly of the Eastern Byzantine rite, all of them composed by bishops with a cosmic and social view of salvation) with the later hymnology expressing the life experience, conflicts and struggles of the monastic communities, but also with the various mystagogical interpretations. More on the relationship between liturgy and mystagogy, ritual and its meaning appears in H.-J. Schultz, *The Byzantine Liturgy: Symbolic Structure and Faith Expression* (Eng. trans.), 1986.

24 Using the anagogic method, Pseudo-Dionysius re-interpreted the liturgical rites of the church by raising them from the letter to the spirit, from the visible acts of the sacraments to the one mystery of the invisible God (cf. E. Boulard, "L'eucharistie d'après le Pseudo-Denys l'Aréopagite", *Bulletin de littérature écclésiastique*, 58, 1957, pp.193-217, and 59, 1958, pp.129-69). Even the bishop's movements within the church are considered as a divine return to the origin of beings. With this method, however, the eschatological view of the eucharist finally disappears. The sole function of worship is now to assist the soul mystically to return to the spiritual realities of the unseen world. The eminent Roman Catholic liturgiologist R. Taft, to whom Eastern liturgical scholarship is heavily indebted (cf. his *The Great Entrance: A History of the Transfer of Gifts and Other Pre-anaphoral Rites of the Liturgy of St John Chrysostom*, 1975, 2d ed. 1978; "How Liturgies Grow: The Evolution of the Byzantine Divine Liturgy", *Orientalia Christiana Periodica*, 43, 1977, p.357ff; *The Liturgy of the Hours in the Christian East*, 1988, etc.), rightly maintains that in the Dionysian system, there is little room for the biblical tradition; the anagogic allegory is the one that dominates. Liturgy is nothing but an allegory of the journey of the soul from the separation and division of sin towards divine communion, through the process of catharsis, enlightenment and wholeness, which are prescribed in the rites. There is very little reference to

Christ's economy on earth, and nothing about his incarnate mediation or his death and resurrection (R. Taft,"The Liturgy of the Great Church", pp.61-62).

For a thorough, critical consideration of the eucharistology of the Areopagite, see R. Roques, *L'univers dionysien: Structure hiérarchique du monde selon le Pseudo-Denys*, 1954). In this system the need for a mediating "hierarchy" thus became inevitable. This reminds us, mutatis mutandis, of Paul's opponents at Colossae and also marks the latent return of a mediatory priesthood in Christian ecclesiology of the East (H. Wybrew, *The Orthodox Liturgy: The Development of the Eucharistic Liturgy in the Byzantine Rite*, 1989; cf. the 1990 SVS press edition with a prologue by Bishop K. Ware, p.115), and especially the West (cf. P.-M. Gy, "Liturgy and Spirituality. II: Sacraments and Liturgy in Latin Christianity", in B. McGinn and J. Meyendorff, eds, *Christian Spirituality. I: Origins to the Twelfth Century*, 1985, pp.365-81). But this was something which according to the fundamental teaching of Hebrews had been abolished *ephapax* (once and for all) by Christ's sacrifice on the cross. According to the late John Meyendorff (*Byzantine Theology: Historical Trends and Doctrinal Themes*, 1974, 2d ed. 1987, p.207), those who followed Dionysian symbolism approached the eucharist in the context of a Hellenistic hierarchical cosmos and understood it as the centre of salvific action through mystical contemplation. That is why there is no mention here at all of Christ's self-sacrifice, nor of his mediatory and high-priestly role (Taft, "The Liturgy of the Great Church", p.62); mediation in the Dionysian system is the work of the earthly hierarchy and the rites that it (and not the community as a whole) performs. Where the Dionysian system reaches its most extreme, however, is in overturning the eschatological and historical dimensions of the eucharist. There is not a single reference to the fundamental Pauline interpretation of the eucharist, according to which at every eucharistic gathering we "proclaim the Lord's death until he comes" (1 Cor. 11:26). Even communion, the most important act of the eucharist, is no more than a symbol of the believer's union with God (*Eccl. Hier.*, 3.3.13). In other words, we have moved from the earlier understanding of the communion of the body of Christ (the incarnate Word) and in the body of Christ (the church) to a communion simply with the pre-existing Logos.

[25] Whereas the allegorical interpretation of the Alexandrians finally did not dominate biblical hermeneutics, their mystagogical (liturgical) interpretation ("anagogic mystagogy") does seem to have prevailed in our liturgical and mission praxis. The alleged influence of the neo-platonic philosophy on the Areopagitic writings is of much lesser importance than its catalytic effect on what we call eucharistic ecclesiology of the church and consequently on spirituality and mission. V. Lossky insists that the orthodoxy of the writings of the Areopagite cannot be questioned (*The Vision of God*, 1983, p.99; cf. also his influential work *The Mystical Theology of the Eastern Church*, 1976). However, all Orthodox theologians who are in favour of a liturgical renewal are critical of the theology of Pseudo-Dionysius (cf. Meyendorff, *Byzantine Theology*, pp.28, 202ff.; G. Florovsky, "Pseudo-Dionyius's Works", in *Religious and Ethical Encyclopedia*, vol. 12, col. 473-80; Schmemann, *Introduction*, pp.150ff., 232ff. etc.; P.Meyendorff, *Saint Germanus of Constantinople on the Divine Liturgy*, 1984).

[26] One should not direct all criticism only against the Alexandrian mystagogical school. The Antiochian school, the other great school of liturgical interpretation in the East, has also contributed, though indirectly, to the abandonment of dynamic horizontal biblical eschatology, with all that this eschatology implies for mission. Its attention was certainly turned more towards history, but not with any strong eschatological perspective, thus interpreting the divine liturgy mainly as a depiction of the Lord's presence on earth.

[27] A. Schmemann, *The Eucharist: Sacrament of the Kingdom*, 1988; also his *The Great Lent: Journey to Pascha*, 1974.

[28] N. Afanassiev, "The Church Which Presides in Love", in *The Primacy of Peter in the Orthodox Church*, collective works by J. Meyendorff, N. Afanassiev, A. Schmemann and N. Kouloumzin, London, 1963, pp.57-110.

[29] R. Taft, "Liturgy and Eucharist I: East", in *Christian Spirituality*, vol. 2, p.417.

[30] Paradoxically, liturgical (corporate/historical/eschatological) spirituality was preserved to some extent within the consciousness of the Orthodox. But this was predominantly outside the actual life of worship, in the daily life of a largely enslaved Orthodoxy, in the secular communities and guilds. The source of this unexpected and happy ending is that the main core of the Sunday eucharistic liturgy, in spite of all the exaggerated symbolism and some unnecessary additions, remained untouched in its communal dimension (eschatological, but vigorously historical and in many ways anti-pietistic). It continued to reflect the understanding of the eucharist primarily as a corporate act of mission that embraces the entire society and the whole created world.

[31] In one of his last contributions A. Schmemann tried to address the issue, cf. his "Symbols and Symbolism in the Byzantine Liturgy: Liturgical Symbols and Their Theological Interpretation", in D. Constantelos, ed., *Orthodox Theology and Diakonia*, 1981, pp.91-102; also in T. Fisch, ed., *Liturgy and Tradition: Theological Reflections of A. Schmemann*, 1990, pp.115-28. He rightly pointed out that "the eucharistic divine liturgy opposed, at least in the essential expressions of its form and spirit, the extremely powerful pressures of the various symbolic interpretations and reductions" (p.125).

[32] On the role of liturgical theology for liturgical reform, cf. the extremely fruitful exchange between A. Schmemann, on the one hand, and B. Botte and W. J. Grisbrooke, on the other (Fisch, *Liturgy and Tradition*, pp.21-47, originally published in *St Vladimir's Theological Quarterly*, 12, 1968, pp.170-74, and 13, 1969, pp.212-24).

[33] In a recent article "Eucharist and Kingdom", *Synaxē*, vol. 49, 51, 52, 1994, pp.7-18, 83-101, 81-97 respectively, Metropolitan of Pergamon John Zizioulas has convincingly shown "how unacceptable it is to undermine and overshadow in many ways the eschatological character of the eucharist both in academic theology and in our liturgical practice" (vol. 52, 1994, p.95).

[34] Most of what follows has already been applied with great success in the liturgical life of the Orthodox monastic communities of New Skete (Cambridge, N.Y.), the great motive for the foundation of which was their "deep and passionate interest in liturgy and its intimate place in Christian life" (*The Divine Liturgy*, New Skete, 1987, p.xiii). Their uniqueness lies in the fact that they "have done a great deal of experimentation... listened carefully to the scholars... [and struggled to] find ways and means of liberating the treasures of Byzantine worship from the paralysis that has tried to suffocate it over the last several centuries" (*ibid.*, pp.xiii-xiv). The brothers of New Skete and their abbot, Archimandrite Laurence, are well aware that "the Eastern churches... are not, generally, prepared to take the necessary plunge into a long-needed liturgical renewal... there seems no way in which a concerted, official movement towards liturgical renewal is about to happen. Individuals and individual communities, therefore, would seem to be the ones to embark on this renewal.... Historically, monasteries have enjoyed the prerogative of such renewal in developing their own usages, and most frequently, their forms were adopted and adapted by the church at large" (*ibid.*, pp.xvff.).

[35] Only then will the sacrament of repentance and the traditional institution of fasting acquire again the significant place they deserve in the spiritual life of the church.

[36] This is what is actually missing from X. S. Papacharalambous's thorough, yet strictly legalistic, treatment of the subject, as clearly indicated by the title of his yet unfinished work "Conditions and Preconditions for Participating in the Divine Eucharist from an Orthodox Perspective", *Scholarly Annual of the Theological School of the University of Athens*, 28, 1993; 29, 1994; 30, 1995; esp.vol. 30, pp.475-546 (to be continued). It is quite interesting how the author is struggling to reach a balanced, compromise solution to the problem. This is yet another example of the necessity of establishing criteria for what actually constitutes an Orthodox viewpoint.

[37] In his recent article "The Liturgical Path of Orthodoxy in America", *St Vladimir's Theological Quarterly*, 40, 1996, pp.43-64, P. Meyendorff vividly reports how successful the experiment of introducing the general confession has been in the Orthodox church in America during the last two decades.

[38] More and more local priests have realized the importance of this for a meaningful worship and the revival of the eucharistic communities. The most painful of all is the exclusion of women (especially in the Greek-speaking churches), even from church singing.

[39] For the last attempt, by St Symeon of Thessaloniki in the 15th century, cf. I. Fountoulis, *The Liturgical Work of Symeon of Thessaloniki* (in Greek), Thessaloniki, 1966.

[40] This need is quite evident in those churches that have recently regained their freedom and still use the old Slavonic, and that realize that the invaluable richness of the Eastern eucharistic tradition has minimal effect on the Orthodox communities and on the world at large. This applies mutatis mutandis also to the Orthodox communities using the ancient Greek.

[41] It is quite a promising sign that a traditional centre of Orthodoxy, like Mount Athos, has been responsible for a corrected edition of the text of the divine liturgy, which among other important details has replaced the established erroneous indication that all eucharistic prayers are to be read "secretly" (*mystikos*) with a neutral one, "the priest prays" (*epeuchetas; Hieratikon A', B', C'*, Monastery of Simonos Petras, 1990ff.; cf also I. Fountoulis, *Divine Liturgies*, Thessaloniki, 1985).

[42] Cf. Matt. 25:31-46, where what really matters is not so much accepting and believing in the abundant love of our triune God (confessional, religious exclusiveness) but exemplifying it to the world through witness (ecclesial inclusiveness).

[43] More on these issues in ch. 3 above, "Mission and Proselytism".

5. New Testament Ecclesiological Perspectives on Laity

The term "laity" designates the state, condition and implications of being a layperson, man or woman, a *laïkos*. In contemporary ecclesiastical usage, however, though the adjective *laïkos* comes etymologically from the noun *laos* (people), its semantic significance is not connected with *laos* in the sense of the people of God. Rather, it always connotes a clear distinction of the layperson from the clergy, the priest and the Levite, designating one who is not qualified from one who is, at least on the level of the most sacred liturgical life. This is the general definition given by theologians, at least from the Roman Catholic side.[1] Even when they define the layperson as "one of the people of God who is not a cleric",[2] even then a clear distinction is presupposed between the clergy and the laity, between the priesthood and the layhood – just as in secular usage the professional is sharply differentiated from the nonprofessional, so the layman or laywoman is the church "amateur". This understanding of the laity, consciously or unconsciously, is derived from the first Christian use of the term by Clement of Rome,[3] where *laïkos* refers to "the part of the people that is neither priestly nor levitical, namely the non-priestly, nonlevitical element among the holy people".[4]

In this short presentation I propose not to follow this rational approach, which presupposes an authoritarian and not an eschatological ecclesiastical structure. This approach assumes some sort of hierarchical structure common to all secular societies and moves from a clear-cut distinction between clergy and laity towards defining and seeking the now lost or forgotten rights or prerogatives of the latter. Instead, I would prefer the "iconological" (i.e. symbolic or analogical) approach, which is the normative Orthodox, biblical and patristic way of looking at the mystery of the church, an integral part of which in all its fullness is the so-called laity. In other words, I suggest that we concentrate on the pro-

• An earlier version of this chapter appeared in the *Scholarly Annual of the Theological School of the University of Thessaloniki*, 29, 1989, pp. 333-56, and is reprinted here by permission of the publisher.

found images of the Christian (i.e. Orthodox) ecclesiology. For it is almost unanimously agreed, even by non-Orthodox, that in all recent explorations of the nature of the church, this great *mysterion*, according to the patristic theology, "does not have a nature that can be readily defined simply by looking, no matter how directly, at the church itself. Its life springs from, is nourished by, and is oriented towards the fullness of glory of the Triune God."[5]

I focus here on the New Testament ecclesiological perspectives on the laity, thus stressing the priority of the biblical consideration of the subject for developing an authentic Orthodox understanding of the mission of the laity. I am totally convinced that as far as methodology is concerned, even with regard to the entire ecclesiological problem, we should not start from later theological images, notions, definitions or interpretations of the mystery of the church, such as the idea of the creation of the church before the creation of the entire universe[6] or the notions of holiness, catholicity etc.[7] Rather, we first should analyze the biblical presuppositions of the Christian ecclesiology – the primary concept of the kingdom of God, Christ's fundamental preaching of the inauguration of the eschatological world, the new heaven and the new earth.[8] And the background of this fundamental preaching clearly is the Old Testament concept of the election *(eklogē)* of God's people *(laos tou theou)* and the unilateral covenant made by God between himself and his own special *(periousios)* people.

It is of fundamental significance in determining the authentic and legitimate ecclesiological presuppositions of Orthodoxy, so important in the ecumenical discussions, that we have full knowledge and a clear view of the historical development of the beginnings of Christian ecclesiology. We cannot grasp the profound meaning of the patristic symbolic language and the Orthodox dogmatic formulations as such unless we know the whole process from Jesus' kerygma to the early Christian community's dynamic interpretation. Then we must move from the major contribution of St Paul (the "body of Christ" image) through the later Pauline (or deutero-Pauline) and Johannine literature onto the Ignatian conception of the church as the eschatological eucharistic assembly with the bishop "in place, and as image, of Christ", surrounded by the presbyters and the entire people of God.

This reference to the biblical period does not represent a fundamentalist appeal to the Bible in order to discover the most ancient – and therefore most authentic – forms of the Christian ecclesiological doctrine. Today it is widely held, even among Protestants, that ancient ecclesiologies, including those recorded in the New Testament, cannot and/or should not be normative for our churches today; they can only be "descriptive and nothing more, and the description should be rigorously separated from interpretation and application".[9] Some others go much further and with extremely sound argumentation contend that the one-ness of the church "cannot be approached on a purely historical level; it can only be laid hold of by faith" as an "eschatological datum".[10] Fur-thermore, such an appeal to the biblical presuppositions is not meant to provide scriptural foundation to the established Orthodox ecclesiology. I hold to the Byzantine hermeneutical principle of "theoptia",[11] which I believe gives new perspectives for the Orthodox understanding of the vocation of the laity.

Let us consider in more detail this process of the development of church studies from Christ to Ignatius, i.e. from the beginnings to the crucial so-called transition point, which eventually established the epis-copocentric nature of the church. Modern New Testament scholarship has abandoned the view that the second-century offices and institutions were a *creatio ex nihilo* but still almost unanimously insists that "it would be extremely dangerous to assume that the second century situa-tions already existed in the first century".[12] Although we meet in the Pas-torals – and only there – Timothy and Titus with the assignment of struc-turing the local communities, it is the notion of *episkopē* (supervision) rather than of *episkopos* that is dealt with in the New Testament, the min-istries of *episkopos* and *presbyteros* being more or less interchangeable. Metropolitan John Zizioulas has convincingly shown that only in the second century was the content and function of *episkopē* clearly defined.[13] It was with the apostolic fathers that the ministry of *episkopos* acquired "its own specific content in relation to other ministries, particu-larly that of the presbyters, and became central to the whole structure of the church".[14] Nevertheless, St Ignatius never thought of a "monarchical episcopacy", as it was wrongly believed by those who were critical of the Orthodox church.[15] His view of the church was purely eschatologi-cal, according to which the local community was an image of the heav-enly structure of the world, in which God reigns. Consequently the bishop's ministry, instead of being historically transmitted,[16] is iconi-cally portrayed in the eschatological community of the divine eucharist. St Ignatius's singling out only one person in the community who would assume the ministry of *episkopē* and who would exercise final authority prevailed in the second century without provoking any negative reaction anywhere because the church understood itself as portraying the kingdom of God on earth. In the local eucharistic gathering the *episkopos* was the "image" (*eikōn*) of Christ surrounded by the *presbyteroi*, who represent the 12 apostles sitting on their eschatological thrones (cf. Matt. 19:28; Luke 22:30).[17]

We return now to the beginnings of the ecclesiological process, namely to *Jesus' preaching*. Without entering into the discussion over the unsolved problem of whether it was the intention of the historical Jesus to establish his own community (so argued on the basis mainly of Matt. 16:18),[18] we can state without any doubt that the fundamental aspect of his preaching was the kingdom of God. Christ inaugurated in his person the new messianic world, which Israel expected at the eschaton. The images that dominate the evangelical tradition are those of the eschatological family (Mark 3:31-35; 10:29-31 par. etc.) or the eschatological banquet (Mark 2:15-17 par.; 6:34-44 par.; 8:1-9; Luke 15), or images that depict Christ as a master (Matt. 10:25) and his pupils as children (Matt. 11:25; cf. Mark 10:24 etc). In other words, they are quite familiar to the images of the contemporary world that point clearly to the idea of the people of God, to whom all the promises of the Old Testament were to be fulfilled at the eschaton.

Exactly the same ecclesiological self-consciousness was developed by the *early Christian community* during the first two decades after Pentecost. During that constructive period the church understood its existence as the authentic expression of the people of God. With a series of terms taken from the Old Testament, the early Christians believed that they were "the Israel of God" (Gal. 6:16), "saints" (Acts 9:32, 41; 26:10; Rom. 1:7; 8:27; 12:13; 15:25 etc.), "the elect" (Rom. 8:33; Col. 3:12 etc.), "a chosen race" and "a royal priesthood" (1 Pet. 2:9) etc. – namely the holy people of God par excellence, to whom all the promises of the book of Exodus (3:12ff.; 19:6) had to be applied.

In order to understand fully the significance of the above biblical terminology for the role of the so-called laity in the church, we have to bear in mind the following:

1. In the Old Testament, God relates to the world by speaking to the community, not to individuals. The traditional belief in Israel was that the human unit in religion was the nation; God was concerned with his people as a nation and cared for the individual, if at all, only through his or her membership in that nation. The covenant at the exodus had been made between the nation and God; the individuals had no direct responsibility for their conduct to God, for it was the concern of the nation as a whole to keep free from sin by observing the covenant. This idea of

corporate personality in religion meant that if other individuals or the nation sinned, all – even the innocent – would be punished indiscriminately. Conversely, individual Israelites had no individual moral responsibility to God, with whom in fact there could be no personal relation. The well-known saying of Jeremiah "The parents have eaten sour grapes, and the children's teeth are set on edge" (Jer. 31:29 [38:29 LXX]), which teaches that one generation necessarily bears the consequences of a previous generation's choices, is quite illuminating. The early church therefore thought of itself primarily as a people, not as a religious organization with various hierarchically structured priestly offices.[19]

2. Another factor that distinguishes the biblical "people" from an organization appears in the secondary and ancillary role of organization within the community. In the ancient polytheistic world political kingship and temple were the very foundation of the social structure. Yet in Israel, despite all attempts of kings and priests to achieve a similar status, neither kingship nor temple possessed the sanctity or the permanence that would enable them to be adequate symbols of the nation's inner life. Israel as the people of God existed before either of them came into being and subsequently continued to exist without them. Israel's golden age was understood to be the era of David and Solomon. The prophets, however, did not appeal to it as the model for community life but instead pointed to the wilderness period, when the bond between people and God was particularly close.[20]

3. An examination of the terminology of both the Old and the New Testaments makes the nature of the church as a people even clearer. The chosen people of God were an *am* (Hebrew, especially in the Prophets) or a *laos* (Greek), whereas the people of the outside world were called *goyim* (Hebrew) or *ethnē* (Greek). The dominant form of expression was that of God choosing or taking a *laos*/*am* from the *ethnē*.[21] For example, during the apostolic synod over the question of Gentiles, Peter described the giving of the Holy Spirit to the Gentiles in the early days of the church's life. James then summed up by saying: "Simeon has related how God first looked favourably on the Gentiles *[ethnē]* to take from among them a people *[laos]* for his name" (Acts 15:14). The same truth is expressed in 1 Pet. 2:10: "Once you were not a people *[laos]*, but now you are God's people *[laos]*."

4. It is quite significant that the first Christian community used the term *ekklēsia* in its Old Testament meaning. It is not accidental that this term as used in the LXX (the Greek translation of the original Hebraic

Old Testament) corresponds to the Hebrew *qahal*, which denotes the congregation of God's people. The Hebrew *edah* (usually translated *synagōgē*, or "community", "assembly") is never rendered as *ekklēsia* in the LXX.[22]

In this primitive period, therefore, the members of the Christian community do not just *belong to* the church, being laymen or laywomen who are simply members of a religious organization administered by priestly orders; rather, they *are* the church.

The second generation after Pentecost is certainly characterized by the great theological contribution of *St Paul*. The apostle takes over the above charismatic notion of the church but gives it in addition a universal and ecumenical character. To the church belong all human beings, Jews and Gentiles, for the latter have been joined to the same tree of the people of God (Rom. 11:13-24). The church, as the new Israel, is thus no longer constituted on grounds of external criteria (circumcision etc.) but on its faith in Jesus Christ ("for not all Israelites truly belong to Israel", Rom. 9:6).

The term, however, with which St Paul recalls the charismatic understanding of the church is *body of Christ*.[23] With this metaphoric expression, St Paul was able to express the charismatic nature of the church by means of the semitic concept of corporate personality. He emphasized that in the church there exists a variety of charismata, exercised by the individual members of the community, laypeople and priest alike, and necessary for the *oikodomē* (building up) and the nutrition of this body, Christ alone being its only head. The consequence of this understanding of the church was St Paul's vigorous defence of, and insistence on, the superiority of his apostolic ministry (cf. 1 Cor. 12:28ff., 2 Cor. 10-12) against any other authority. It is of utmost importance that at this decisive period of formation of Christian theology, this great figure of Christianity was completely convinced that he was "an apostle – sent neither by human commission nor from human authorities, but through Jesus Christ and God the Father" (Gal. 1:1). On this basis, St Paul was questioning the exclusive authority of any leading group, either from the circle of the Twelve or generally of the Jerusalem community.

The *Johannine* image of the vine (John 15:1-8) is equally impressive. As with the Pauline term *soma* (body), the double scheme *ampelosklēmata* (vine-branch) indicates the special relationship between Christ and the people of God, which reveals the inner basis of ecclesial life. Christ is the vine, the individual members of the community are the vine-branches, and God is the vine-dresser. The branches bear fruit, but they are able to do so only because they remain on the vine. The worthless branches are cut away and burned, whereas the rest are pruned so that they may bear more fruit. The only criterion of belonging to the church is the bearing of much fruit, and thereby God the Father is glorified (v.8).[24]

Most of the other New Testament figures for the church – "household of faith" (Eph. 2:11-21), "fellowship" (1 Cor. 1:9 etc), "new covenant" (2 Cor. 3:6 etc), "bride of Christ" (Eph. 5:31-32; Rev. 21:9), "little flock" (Luke 12:32 etc.) – all point to the same conception: namely that the new community is a *people*, bound together, not by external structures of organization, but by the Holy Spirit, who proceeds from God the Father and is sent by Christ. It is certainly true that later – certainly within the period of the composition of the New Testament writings – this charismatic community acquired some kind of structure with certain offices, and it developed some sort of ecclesiastical authority, the bearers of which were entitled to preserve the apostolic heritage and to distinguish correct teaching (the *parakatathēkē*, "deposit", as it is called in the Pastorals) from false. One can also argue that the church, even from the very beginning, has never lived without "order".[25] However, it never deviated to an institutionalism, nor did it lose its prophetic and charismatic character or its consciousness of being a people. It is exactly for this reason that it did not derive its inner structure from the Jewish priestly system; rather, it developed into a eucharistic episcopocentric system, which is a completely different matter.

These are, very briefly, the most characteristic images used by the church at the beginning of its life. The two major aspects emphasized during this period are the *christological* and the *pneumatological* – the importance of the person of Christ and the idea of the koinonia, which is by definition (2 Cor. 13:13) the domain of the Holy Spirit. We can therefore say that New Testament ecclesiology revolves around the same problem that confronts our present Orthodox theology. According to Metropolitan J. Zizioulas, the problem of "how to relate the institutional with the charismatic, the Christological with the pneumatological aspects of ecclesiology, still awaits its treatment by Orthodox theology".[26]

We can overcome this dilemma, however, by focusing instead on the motif that dominates the entire New Testament literature from the very first document (1 Thessalonians) – the *eschatological dimension* as it colours New Testament ecclesiology overall. It is quite significant to know that even the Pauline image "body of Christ", the most christocentric of all, was originally set against the background of the charismata of the Holy Spirit (1 Corinthians 12-14). Conversely, it is not an accident that the two main eucharistic references in 1 Corinthians have a lot in common with this ecclesiological image (cf. "this is my body", 11:24; and "the bread we break, is it not sharing in the body of Christ? Because there is one bread, we who are many are one body", 10:16-17). If we now take into account that St Paul understands the eucharist (which by definition is the mystery of the church, not a mystery in the church) as a proclamation "of the Lord's death until he comes" (11:26), then this eschatological understanding of the church becomes quite evident. This understanding of the church is evidenced throughout the whole apostolic and post-apostolic literature. I will confine myself only to the decisive stages of the ecclesiological process.

In *Colossians* and *Ephesians*, where we have more advanced ecclesiological statements with the introduction of the concept of the "head" (Christ) of the body, it is stated that the church "is [Christ's] body, the fullness of him who fills all in all" (Eph. 1:23). In *Acts* where a synthesis between the historical and the eschatological realities, the "already" and the "not yet" of the kingdom of God, has been attempted, the period of the church, which is in fact the period of the Holy Spirit, is expressedly conceived as belonging to the eschaton (2:17). Without removing the tension between history and the eschaton, the book of Acts presents the church as the iconological manifestation of the kingdom of God in the concrete structure of the collegium of the 12 apostles (1:13-26).

In *Hebrews* the eschatological dimension of the christological aspect of the church is developed in a quite new perspective. The clause "remember your leaders *[hēgoumenoi]*" (13:7) is connected with the significant statement "Jesus Christ is the same yesterday and today and forever" (v.8) which is ecclesiological, not christological. There is no division of the eucharistic community into "orders", i.e. into categories or classes of people; neither is there any distinction between the priesthood and the laity. The "leaders" as the expression of the church are nothing but the eschatological image of Christ and his projection to the end of time. A little later in the book of *Revelation* the eschatological character of the church is depicted in the image of the heavenly worship of the Lamb, surrounded by the 24 presbyters (ch. 4-5). The clue for decoding this symbolic number is found in 21:12-14, where it becomes clear that they represent the 12 tribes of Israel plus the 12 apostles – the former Israel and the new Israel, God's people in its totality. Here the old apocalyptic picture of the eschatological judgment (cf. Matt. 19:28 = Luke

22:30; also 1 Cor. 6:2) is transformed into a worshiping eschatological gathering. The ecclesiology of Revelation is thus only a step short of the Ignatian concept of the church as a eucharistic community with the bishop as the image of Christ surrounded by the presbyters, being the image of the apostles, and the entire people of God.[27]

The whole process, therefore, from Jesus' preaching to the Ignatian theology reveals that primarily the *eschatological* dimension of the church was stressed, not the hierarchical (which would imply a division into ministries and orders, into clergy and laity). The early Christian community understood itself as portraying the kingdom of God on earth. Similarly, the primary concern of the great theologians of the apostolic and post-apostolic period was to maintain clearly the vision of that kingdom before the eyes of the people of God. Having said that, I do not insist on the exclusiveness of this parameter; for no single image or overall consideration can exhaust the reality of the church as a whole. We cannot deny, however, the priority of the kingdom of God in all ecclesiological considerations. In the early church everything belonged to the kingdom. The church did not administer all reality; it only prepared the way to that kingdom. By being the body of Christ, the church understood itself as the manifestation of Christ's own ministry (which was beyond any doubt centred on the kingdom) and its projection to the world.

It was for this reason, I suppose, that the early church applied to Christ all forms of ministry, seeing him as apostle (Heb. 3:1), prophet (Matt. 23:8, John 13:13), priest (Heb. 5:6; 8:4; 10:21 etc.), bishop (1 Pet. 2:25), shepherd (1 Pet. 5:4-5; Heb. 13:20), deacon (Rom. 15:8; Luke 22:27; Phil. 2:7). The church understood its own ministries not as parallel to but as identical with those of Christ. The bishop, for example, is a *typos* (model, figure) of Christ, not an ambassador of Christ.

This understanding by the early Christian community in the apostolic and post-apostolic period of the nature of the church as a communion-event of an eschatological character, oriented towards the kingdom of God, has been experienced during the long history of Orthodoxy nowhere better than within the context of the divine eucharistic liturgy. The reason why the Eastern churches in the past have scarcely experienced the problem of clericalism and anti-clericalism or antagonism between clergy and laity is precisely that Orthodoxy has understood all ministries (above all, the sacramental priesthood) always within the context of the community.[28] This understanding was the inevitable result of the *eschatological* vision of the eucharistic ecclesiology.

NOTES

[1] Roman Catholic theology was seriously concerned with this problem three decades ago; cf. e.g. Y.M.J. Congar, *Lay People in the Church* (Eng. trans.), 1965.

[2] M. Jourjon, "Les premiers emplois du mot 'laïc' dans la littérature patristique", *Lumière et vie*, 65, 1963, pp.37ff.

[3] "Special ministries have been assigned to the high priest, a special place has been alloted to the priests, and the Levites have their own duties. Laypeople are bound by rules laid down for the laity" (1 Clem. 40:5).

[4] M. Jourjon, "Les premiers emplois", cf. I. de la Potterie, "L'origine et le sens primitif du mot 'laïc'", *Nouvelle revue théologique*, 60, 1958, pp.840ff.

[5] P.S. Minear, *Images of the Church in the New Testament*, 1960, p.12.

[6] Cf. e.g. the elaboration of this doctrine by St Maximus the Confessor.

[7] I refer to the well-known article of the Nicene-Constantinopolitan Creed.

[8] Cf. the interesting description by St John in Revelation 21:1ff.

[9] P.S. Minear, "Ontology and Ecclesiology in the Apocalypse", *New Testament Studies*, 13, 1965, pp.89ff. Cf. also Metropolitan J. Zizioulas's comment on a similar situation: "We must not venerate history in a conservativistic manner. So what the first three centuries did is not obligatory for the church today" ("Episkope and Episkopos in the Early Church: A Brief Survey of the Evidence," in *Episkope and the Episkopate in Ecumenical Perspective*, Faith and Order paper 102, Geneva, 1980, pp.30ff.).

[10] E. Käsemann, "Unity and Diversity in New Testament Ecclesiology", *Novum Testamentum*, 6, 1963, pp.290ff.

[11] Cf. J. Meyendorff, *Byzantine Theology: Historical Trends and Doctrinal Themes*, 1974, pp.8ff.

[12] R.E. Brown, "A Brief Survey of the New Testament Evidence on Episkope and Episkopos", in *Episkope and Episkopate*, pp.l5ff.

[13] Zizioulas, "Episkope and Episkopos", p.30.

[14] *Ibid.*

[15] Cf. e.g. H. Lietzmann, *Geschichte der alten Kirche*, 1961, p.264.

[16] It is important to note that Ignatius did not share Clement's view of a linear, historical transmission of ministry from God through Christ to the apostles and finally to bishops and deacons (1 Clem. 42) but instead held a more eschatological view of the church as a "eucharistic community". R.E. Brown considers Clement's theological analysis as an oversimplification ("A Brief Survey", p.29).

[17] Zizioulas, "Episkope and Episkopos", p.33.

[18] Since the whole issue is still debated, I can only refer to the compromising view of R. Schnackenburg that the idea of the church is a later form (Spätform) of Jesus' authentic thought (*Gottes Herrschaft und Reich. Eine biblisch-theologische Studie*, 1959).

[19] Cf. E. Wright et al., *The Biblical Doctrine of Man in Society*, 1954, pp.22ff.

[20] *Ibid.*, pp.79-80.

[21] *Ibid.*, p.22.

[22] Cf. W. Schrage, "Ekklesia und Synagoge. Zum Ursprung des urchristlichen Kirchenbegriffs", *Zeitschrift für Theologie und Kirche*, 60, 1963, pp.178ff.

[23] Cf. P. Vassiliadis, "Ecclesiological Views of St Paul" (in Greek), in *Biblical Hermeneutical Studies*, 1988, pp.395ff.

[24] Wright, *The Biblical Doctrine*, pp.80-81.

[25] E. Lohse, *Grundriss der neutestamentlichen Theologie*, 1974, § 37.

[26] Zizioulas, *Being as Communion*, p.125.

[27] P. Vassiliadis, "*Eikon* and *Ekklesia* in the Apocalypse", in *Greek Orthodox Theological Review*, 38, 1993. pp. 103-17, and *Biblical Hermeneutical Studies*, pp.414ff.

[28] Zizioulas, *Being as Communion*, pp.204ff.

6. Your Will Be Done:
Reflections from St Paul

One of the most puzzling questions that Christians all over the world ask today concerns the way they should be doing God's will in their lives and in the life of their societies. In the long history of our church, people have tried in very many ways to reflect upon the important petition of our Lord's prayer: "Your will be done, on earth as it is in heaven" (Matt. 6:10). The question remains, though, in view of rapidly changing society and the different social, political and economic structures. From the very beginning of Christianity, certainly since Jerome's time, this basic prayer of the church has been clearly understood as an eschatological prayer. It is most likely for this reason that *Cathechismus Romanus*, probably following Origen,[1] connected the final clause ("on earth as it is in heaven") with the first three petitions: "hallowed be your name," "your kingdom come," "your will be done." Christian behaviour, therefore, as it reflects "God's will," has to be seen in close relation to the kingdom of God, this new world, "a new heaven and a new earth," which St John described in Revelation (21:1ff.).

I propose to give an account of St Paul's reflection on this very important, and yet neglected and sometimes misinterpreted, petition of our Lord's prayer; after all, his views are in fact the earliest and most dynamic interpretation of Christ's earthly kerygma as it is recorded in the gospel of St Matthew. I focus on Paul because this great thinker and father of Christian theology is accused from various quarters of de-radicalizing the words of the historical Jesus and the kerygma of the early church. In addition, even among professional theologians there is a tendency, especially since the time of the Reformation, to determine St Paul's theology exclusively on grounds of the old *sola fide* justification theory. This theory, significant as it is, has in effect pushed into the background the incarnational/social aspects of his teaching. Using the results of the most recent scholarly research on the analysis of the Pauline data,

● An earlier version of this chapter appeared in *International Review of Mission*, 75, 1989, pp.376-82.

I hope to show how unjust this consideration is by examining the real meaning of the most significant parameters of his dogmatic and ethical teaching, namely his *theology of the cross* and his teaching on *collection*, as these express his doctrine of salvation and his understanding of Christian love.

St Paul is rightly considered as the father of the Christian doctrine of salvation. His numerous references to Jesus' death as an act of salvation have undoubtedly determined the basic soteriological concept of Christianity. It was not until the period of scholastic theology, however, that the first attempt at a systematic exposition of this important Christian doctrine occurred. It was the time, following the eventual split between Eastern and Western Christianity, that Anselm of Canterbury put forward his well-known "satisfaction theory". In his famous work *Cur Deus Homo?* he attempted to show the necessity of Christ's incarnation and death on the cross for the salvation of humankind on the basis of a juridical relationship between people and God. The divine justice, he believed, because of human disobedience, demanded a *satisfactio* that human beings alone were unable to fulfil; therefore, God took, in God's own self, the penalty of crucifixion.[2]

Anselm's theory, which had a catalytic effect upon the development of all of Western theology and culture,[3] in fact transferred the decisive point of salvation from the incarnation – and the whole divine economy – to the specific moment of Jesus' death on the cross. From then on, soteriology shifted away from Christology and gradually became a separate chapter in dogmatic theology. This, however, was not the way the early undivided church considered soteriology. In the golden age of patristic theology the soteriological problem was inter-related with the christological one. The early fathers answered the question of salvation in close relation to – in fact as a consequence of – the Christian doctrine of the nature, essence and energies of the second person of the Holy Trinity.

It is widely held that Christian theology, with its classic *extra nos – pro nobis* soteriology, has played a decisive role in the establishment of our Western culture, which was in fact due to the passive role the Christian church played in socio-politico-economical developments. But the Christian dogma of salvation depends very much upon the soteriological statements and the interpretative references to Jesus' death, which are found in the *corpus paulinum*, especially in St Paul's great epistles. Today the discussion on the concept of *extra nos – pro nobis* has been reopened with a trend to question its validity, or at least its centrality, in the theology of St Paul.[4]

A number of New Testament scholars from all Christian quarters have tried in recent years to analyze the origin of the theological significance of Jesus' death.[5] They all illustrate that there was no unanimity among the first Christians with regard to the interpretation of Jesus' death on the cross. In fact, there was a considerable variety of attempts to give a theological interpretation to Jesus' death.[6]

Besides the so-called soteriological interpretation, according to which the raison d'être of Jesus' death on the cross was the salvation of humankind, one can count at least another four crystallized interpretative attempts, with which the early Christian community was trying to grasp the mystery of the crucifixion. One was the *prophetic* interpretation, traces of which are found in the earliest Pauline epistle (1 Thess. 2:15), Acts (7:52), the Marcan tradition (cf. Mark 12:1-12 par) and the Q-document. According to this interpretation Jesus' death was given no expiatory significance. Rather, it was seen as the true continuation of the persecution, sufferings and violent end of the Old Testament prophets.

Another interpretation was the *dialectic*, found in the earliest and most traditional strata of Acts (2:23-31, 32-36; 3:15; 4:10; 5:30; 10:39-40) and the Pauline literature (1 Thess. 4:14; Rom. 8:34; 14:9a; 2 Cor. 13:4). According to this interpretation Jesus' death is dialectically contrasted (J. Roloff calls it *Kontrastschema*)[7] with the resurrection, with the stress on the latter, thus making no soteriological hint to the cross.

A third interpretation was the *apocalyptic* (or *eschatological*), to be found in the synoptic passion predictions (Mark 8:31 par.; 9:31 par.; 10:33 par.). Here, too, Jesus' death is referred to as having no soteriological significance, but as an eschatological act in full agreement with the divine plan.

Finally, there is the *eucharistic* or *covenantal* interpretation. The earliest layers of the eucharistic tradition both in Paul and in the synoptic gospels (1 Cor. 11:25 par.) seem to point to other than the expiatory significance of Jesus' death. His blood, rather, has sealed the new covenant that God established with the Christian church (cf. also Mark 10:45a; Luke 12:37b, 22:37b).

The almost unanimous preference in the later New Testament literature for the so-called *soteriological* interpretation does not reflect the plurality of the theological thinking of the first Christian generation. This fifth interpretative attempt of the early church can surely be traced to the period before St Paul's conversion (cf. 1 Cor. 15:3ff.), which means that it was crystallized even during the first decade after the interpreted event. The lack of any reference in other pre-Pauline strata of the early Christian tradition, however, would suggest a limited usage in the early Christian community. In contrast, the prophetic interpretation, traces of which are found in almost all layers of primitive Christianity (Q-community, Hellenistic community, Marcan community, Pauline community), suggests that it was widespread during this creative period. Nevertheless, its complete absence from the later stages of New Testament literature, as well as the establishment of the soteriological interpretation, points to a continuous development and reinterpretation of this most significant event of the divine economy in the early church. In my view, the predominant place the soteriological interpretation had in later New Testament literature is due to its Hellenistic background, compared with the more or less Judaic background of all the other interpretations.

If we want to discover St Paul's real contribution to the early Christian soteriology and grasp the true perspectives of his understanding of salvation, we should turn to the above sketched variety of interpretations of Jesus' death in the early church. It is worth noting that almost all pre-Pauline interpretations of Jesus' death are hinted at in the undisputed epistles of St Paul. Our great apostle preserves, and to a certain extent accepts, all the traditional interpretations. Not only does he refuse to reject any of the previous interpretations, but also, as E. Käsemann rightly observes,[8] he does not even show his preference for any of them, even the soteriological one, which no doubt seems to prevail in the *corpus paulinum*.

A quick glance at the terminology used by St Paul in his effort to clarify the special character of Jesus' death on the cross shows some slight change in the centre of gravity of the early Christian soteriology. There may be some objections to the real meaning of the ransom terminology in Paul. One can even argue that it is not absolutely clear whether the sacrificial, the juridical, or the conciliatory terminology, with which the mystery of salvation is expressed in the Pauline epistles, comes from St Paul himself or expresses the faith of the first Christian community. What no one can deny is that the theological meaning attached to *stauros* (cross) and its cognates constitutes one of the most characteristic features of St Paul's theology. The "word of the cross" has become for St Paul the decisive parameter that gave new perspective to the traditional understanding of Jesus' death, especially to the soteriological *extra nos – pro nobis* interpretation.[9] This new perspective is determined by the significance (in the negative sense) that this capital punishment had in pre-Christian times.[10] It was St Paul who transformed this most terrible, disgracing and humiliating symbol in contemporary Roman society into the element of the divine economy with the most significance (in the positive sense). In that sense *stauros* is the centre of the Pauline soteriology. More precisely, our great apostle, while accepting the various traditional interpretations of this greatest event of the earthly ministry of our Lord, any time his opponents (of Judaizing, enthusiastic or libertine tendency) challenged his gospel, he reinterpreted the significance of Jesus' death on the basis of his theory of the cross, with all the socio-political consequences this humiliating symbol connotated in contemporary Roman society.

If St Paul's theology of the cross, the heart of his dogmatic theology, had such sociological connotations, one would normally expect his ethical teaching and missionary activity to follow the same line. And this is certainly the case; the most representative side of his praxis, which in this respect can easily serve as a test case, is undoubtedly his *collection project*. Indeed, no aspect of his missionary endeavour occupies more place in St Paul's thought and activity, and this is manifestly reflected in his great epistles. While his teaching on salvation, especially the justification-by-faith aspect of his soteriology, has been examined in the recent past in much detail, the sociological/incarnational dimension of his theology, as well as his multifarious missionary practice, remain dangerously neglected areas in modern New Testament scholarship.[11] Even in the rare cases where New Testament scholarly research deals with relevant subjects (e.g. the Pauline collection), so one-sided is the theological emphasis that very seldom do we encounter a balanced treatment.[12]

Let us examine the relevant New Testament data. All four great, undisputed epistles of St Paul contain a clear reference to the collection (cf. Gal. 2:10; 1 Cor. 16:1-4; 2 Corinthians 8-9; Rom. 15:25-32).[13] These passages convey several messages. (1) St Paul considered the collection project to be the only important decision of the apostolic council, with of course the exception of the division of missionary territories. (2) The collection project was well organized, thus occupying an important place in St Paul's itinerary; his entire third missionary trip was devoted almost exclusively to the transfer of the collection to Jerusalem.[14] (3) In St Paul's thinking the collection project was connected both to the dogmatic teaching of the Christian community (cf. 2 Cor. 8:9) and to the early church's worship (cf. 1 Cor. 16:2; 2 Cor. 9:11-15); it was identified with a true and spiritual liturgy. (4) Whatever the origin of the collection project,[15] or whatever may be its connection with the so-called Antiochean collection (Acts 11:27-30; 12:25),[16] it was St Paul who attached special theological significance to the collection. (5) The Pauline collection certainly had ecumenical,[17] ecclesiological and eschatological characteristics. No doubt it was seen as the tangible token of the unity of the church, presenting irrefutable evidence that God was calling the Gentiles to faith; it can also be considered as an eschatological pilgrimage of the Gentile Christians to Jerusalem.[18] Above all, however, it was meant to cover social purposes.[19] Its final goal, according to St Paul's thinking, was the social ideal of the *equal distribution and communion of material wealth*. Using a wide variety of terms to describe the collection project (*charis, koinonia, diakonia, leitourgia, eucharistia* etc.), St Paul understood the collection as the social response of the body of Christ, the church, to God's will. For him it was the inevitable response to the kingdom of God, the new world inaugurated by Jesus Christ our Lord.

It is undeniable that this very significant project of the early church, in today's ecclesiastical practice, both Eastern and Western, has lapsed into an underemphasized institution, one deprived of the social and ecumenical dimension that St Paul gave it.

G. Theissen, whose superb sociological studies on the situation in the early church offered new insights and opened new horizons in New Testament scholarship,[20] has convincingly argued that St Paul developed a new ethos in social life, obviously different from that of both the synoptic and the Johannine traditions: the ethos of primitive Christian-love patriarchalism. This ethos, which on the one hand demanded from the members of the society a high degree of solidarity and brotherliness, but on the other preserved almost intact the various social strata, resulted in the church's immense success over the ruins of the ancient world.[21] I argued above that the ultimate goal of the Pauline collection, a project that occupied a far greater part in the early church's activity than the one presupposed in Acts, was in the long term the equal distribution and the sharing of material wealth. If we now take Theissen's views a step further, we come to the following conclusion:

The above solution, offered by St Paul to the ancient society, might not have been so idealistic as the communal life of the Palestinian community experience (synoptic tradition/Acts); it might also have been different from the radical mysticism of the Johannine community. Nevertheless, it was the only realistic solution that not only made a lasting impact on later Christianity but also guided the fathers of the church to fight for social justice.[22]

* * *

We may summarize as follows the quintessence of St Paul's dynamic interpretation of the third petition of our Lord's prayer: "Your will be done." His theology of the cross and his teaching on collection, expressing both the dogmatic/theoretical and the ethical/practical aspects of his theology, manifest in a clear and indisputable manner the way in which he understood "mission in Christ's way".[23] It cannot be accidental that John Chrysostom too, considered the best interpreter of St Paul, understood in exactly the same way the words of our Lord: "Your will be done." In his comments on Matthew 6:10 he wrote:

> And again he had ordered each one of us who pray to take upon himself the care of the whole world [*oecumene*]. For he did not at all say, "Your will be done" in me or in us but everywhere on earth, so that error may be destroyed, and truth implanted, and all wickedness cast out, and virtue return, and no difference in this respect be henceforth between heaven and earth.[24]

NOTES

[1] *On Blessing*, 26.2.

[2] For a comprehensive analysis of this influential theory of Anselm and a critique of his main thesis, see H. Kessler, *Die theologische Bedeutung des Todes Jesu: Eine traditionsgeschichtliche Untersuchung*, Dusseldorf, 1970.

[3] Cf. A. Sabbatier, *The Doctrine of the Atonement* (Eng. trans.), London, 1904, p.69.

[4] Cf. among others P. Vassiliadis, *Cross and Salvation: The Soteriological Background of St Paul's Teaching about the Cross in the Light of the Pre-Pauline Interpretation of Jesus' Death* (in Greek), Thessaloniki, 1983, for the Orthodox world; O. Knoch, "Zur Diskussion über die Heilsbedeutung des Todes Jesu", *Theologisches Jahrbuch, 1977-78*, Leipzig, 1978, pp.250ff., for the Catholic world; and P. Viering, *Der Kreuzestod Jesu: Interpretation eines Gutachtens*, Gütersloh, 1969, for the German-speaking Protestant world.

[5] Apart from Kessler, *Die theologische Bedeutung des Todes Jesu*, cf. K. Kertelge, ed., *Der Tod Jesu: Deutungen im Neuen Testament*, Freiburg, 1976; G. Delling, *Der Kreuzestod Jesu in der urchristlichen Verkündigung*, Göttingen, 1972; M. Hengel, *The Atonement: The Origins of the Doctrine in the New Testament*, Philadelphia, 1981; F.-J. Ortkemper, *Das Kreuz in der Verkündigung des Apostels Paulus dargestellt an den Texten der paulinischen Hauptbriefe*, Stuttgart, 1967; J. Roloff, "Anfange der soteriologischen Deutung des Todes Jesu (Mk X.45 und Lk XXII.27)", *New Testament Studies*, 19, 1972, pp.38-64; and M.-L. Gubler, *Die frühesten Deutungen des Todes Jesu: Eine motivgeschichtliche Darstellung auf Grund der neueren exegetische Forschung*, Fribourg, 1977; and Vassiliadis, *Cross and Salvation*.

[6] Vassiliadis, *Cross and Salvation*, pp.47ff.

[7] Roloff, "Anfange der soteriologischen Deutung", p.39.

[8] E. Käsemann, "Die Heilsbedeutung des Todes Jesu nach Paulus", in F. Viering, ed., *Zur Bedeutung des Todes Jesu: Exegetische Beiträge*, Gütersloh, 1967, pp.11-34.

[9] According to Kertelge, "For Paul the word of the cross, i.e. of the Crucified, is not merely a variation of the traditional view of Jesus' atoning death but, in certain respects, its radicalization" ("Das Verständnis des Todes Jesu bei Paulus", in his *Der Tod Jesu*, p.125).

[10] I refer to the classic treatment by H. Fulda, *Das Kreuz und die Kreuzigung*, Breslau, 1878; and J. Blinder, *Der Prozess Jesu*, Regensburg, 1969; cf. also M. Hengel, "Mors turpissima crucis: Die Kreuzigung in der antiken Welt und die 'Torheit' des 'Wortes vom Kreuz'", in *Rechtfertigung. Festschrift für E. Käsemann*, Tübingen, 1976, pp.25-84.

[11] More in my book *Charis – Koinonia – Diakonia: The Social Character of the Pauline Collection* (Introduction and Commentary on 2 Cor. 8-9) (in Greek), Thessaloniki, 1985.

[12] The best-known studies on collection are those by D. Georgi, *Die Geschichte der Kollekte des Paulus für Jerusalem*, Hamburg, 1965 (now also in English: *Remembering the Poor: The History of Paul's Collection for Jerusalem*, Nashville, 1992); and K.F. Nickle, *The Collection: A Study in Paul's Strategy*, London, 1966. They both have contributed considerably to the understanding of St Paul's view on the matter.

[13] For other indirect references in the New Testament on the subject, cf. Acts 11:27-30; 12:25; 24:17, 26; Heb. 6:10; also Rom. 1:13; 12:13; Eph. 4:28; 2 Thess. 3:13; 1 Tim. 5:16; 6:18; Tit. 3:8, 14; Heb. 13:16; James 1:27; 2:2-7; 1 Pet. 4:10-11; 1 John 3:17; 3 John 5-6.

[14] In Acts all references to the Pauline collection are downplayed, distorted or even silenced; this is due to theological motivations or purposes.

[15] Even if we accept that the Pauline collection was modelled after the Jewish half-shekel temple tax, it is abundantly clear that St Paul made this project a unique phenomenon in world history, both religious and social.

[16] In view of the theological character of the book of Acts, it is quite possible that the Antiochean account was modelled after the Pauline project, rather than vice versa.

[17] Cf. Georgi, *Die Geschichte der Kollekte*, p.80.

[18] Cf. Nickle, *The Collection*, pp.142-43.

[19] Cf. L.E. Keck, "The Poor among the Saints in the New Testament", *Zeitschrift für die neutestamentliche Wissenschaft*, 56, 1965, pp.100-29; and C.K. Barrett, *A Commentary on the Second Epistle to the Corinthians*, London, 1973, p.27.

[20] Cf. G. Theissen, *The Social Setting of Pauline Christianity* (Eng. trans.), Philadelphia, 1979.

[21] Theissen, "Social Stratification in the Corinthian Community", in *ibid.*, pp.69-119, esp. pp.107ff.

[22] Cf. J. Petrou, *Social Justice: The Problem of Social Justice in the Orthodox Tradition* (in Greek), Thessaloniki, 1992.

[23] Cf. the WCC report "Mission and Evangelism: An Ecumenical Affirmation", *International Review of Mission*, 71, 1982, pp.427-51.

[24] John Christostom, Homily 19 on Matthew, *Patrologiae graeca*, 57, col. 280.

7. God's Will for His People: A Bible Study on Deuteronomy 6:20-25

The book of Deuteronomy, which in its present form is most likely the final product of a long and complex process of growth, consists almost exclusively of three long speeches (1:6-4:40; 5:1-28:68; 29:2-30:20) addressed by Moses to the Israelites, God's chosen people, as they were standing on the plain of Canaan. Among the admonitions of the second and more significant of Moses' addresses, we read the following:

> When your children ask you in time to come, "What is the meaning of the decrees and the statutes and the ordinances that the Lord our God has commanded you?" then you shall say to your children, "We were Pharaoh's slaves in Egypt, but the Lord brought us out of Egypt with a mighty hand. The Lord displayed before our eyes great and awesome signs and wonders against Egypt, against Pharaoh and all his household. He brought us out from there in order to bring us in, to give us the land that he promised on oath to our ancestors. Then the Lord commanded us to observe all these statutes, to fear the Lord our God, for our lasting good, so as to keep us alive, as is now the case. If we diligently observe this entire commandment before the Lord our God, as he has commanded us, we will be in the right." (Deut. 6:20-25)

Why did the Lord our God command us to obey these laws? (6:20) At first glance this text appears to be somehow irrelevant to our faith, as its main content is about law and commands. Even more so if it is read against the background of world Christian mission. This is almost true, but not quite. For the entire book of Deuteronomy, together with the rest of the so-called deuteronomistic traditions, constitutes the most important tradition for understanding the law as God's will for his people. After all, there is no book more important for the understanding of the New Testament, and consequently for grasping the true meaning of Christian mission, than Deuteronomy.

• An earlier version of this chapter appeared in *International Review of Mission*, 77, 1988, pp.179-84.

In Deuteronomy Moses is presented not as a mere legislator but as teacher and expositor of God's will (cf. 1:5). The written statutes and ordinances are therefore given as a sermonic appeal to do God's will in a concrete situation of life (cf. Deut. 12:26 with Ex. 20:23). The main emphasis therefore falls on love. It can be argued that the law in Deuteronomy is an explication of what it means to love God. Loving God with all one's heart and soul and might which is repeatedly commanded in Deuteronomy (cf. 6:5, the famous *shema*, "hear"; 10:12; 11:1ff.; 19:9; 30:6-10, etc.), means accepting God as the sovereign over the whole of life. That is why all kinds of law are found in Deuteronomy – not only religious laws, concerning worship, festivals, idolatry, offerings, clean and unclean food, priests and prophets, but also laws for family life, sexual activity, financial transactions; even laws regulating the conduct of war. No area of Israel's life is excluded from legislation because Israel's commitment must be a total commitment.

First, the basic idea of Deuteronomy is the conception of the covenant (which is also emphasized in the earlier pentateuchal traditions) as God's loving election of Israel (based on a J idea) and of the law as Israel's loyal response to that election. We have to bear in mind that although Deuteronomy was written in the time of monarchy and therefore one would normally expect it to make room for the kingship, in fact it subordinates the king to the covenant law, placing him on a level with every other Israelite.

... your children will ask you... then tell them (6:20-21). Another emphasis of Deuteronomy, as is exemplified in our text, is that this response of Israel to God's election must be personal, it must be made by every individual of every generation. Doing God's will is a matter of personal responsibility. Deuteronomy's concern, in addition, is that all understand God's words. Deuteronomy actually aims at the hearts and minds and wills of its readers. Its appeal is a personal one, and for this reason the singular is used. It confronts the audience with no false appeal to authority of power or office, and no moralistic demand to obedience is made without thinking. In Christian mission everything has to be explained and made comprehensible to ordinary people, especially to younger generations.

More important, however, for the Christian mission is that the main concept of Deuteronomy is not just the affirmation of the idea of the covenant; it is also and mainly its *renewal*. It may not be accidental that this book came down to us through the LXX translation as a *deutero-nomion*, namely as a second – and therefore reinterpreted, or properly interpreted – law; and this is not just a mistaken rendering of "copy" in 17-18. In this book the legal tradition of the book of Exodus (e.g. the covenant code or the decalogue) is not just repeated; it is reinterpreted in contemporary terms, so that the promises and demands of the covenant are brought near to every worshiping Israelite.

The Lord rescued us... he brought us out from Egypt (6:22-23). Of even greater importance is the close connection between God's will and God's mighty work, between lawgiving and Passover, both of which must be passed on from generation to generation, from father to son.

A special emphasis in Deuteronomy is that God's revelation to humankind to the entire world is presented functionally, not ontologically. God makes himself known to his chosen people, and through them to the whole world, by what God has done in their lives. They were slaves of the king of Egypt, and God rescued them by his great power; with their own eyes they saw God work miracles and do terrifying things to the Egyptians. God is not found by a mystical escape to a spiritual realm. People know God because he confronts them by his action. Only with such a background can we rightly conceive the meaning of the law. And going further, Deuteronomy understands salvation in a very concrete way: here salvation primarily concerns liberation from slavery, from all sorts of slavery. That is why Christian mission cannot be limited to evangelizing the world by preaching liberation only from spiritual bonds, leaving aside or scandalously ignoring the political, economical, cultural, ideological oppression of God's creation in his very image of humanity. It was against this background that Christ in his inaugural proclamation of his gospel applied to himself Isaiah's prophecy: "The Spirit of the Lord is upon me, because he has anointed me to bring good news to the poor. He has sent me to proclaim release to the captives... to let the oppressed go free" (Luke 4:18).

One of the most distinctive characteristics of Deuteronomy – in fact of the entire biblical tradition – is that Israel's theology of law was determined by its theology of history. Unlike its neighbours, Israel had no separate and autonomous legal code. Its law was always an inseparable part of the history of salvation. In fact, the most revered part of the Old Testament – the *torah*, the Pentateuch – is nothing more than a record of how Israel became a nation. And Deuteronomy among the books of the *torah* cannot be identified with pure legalism; nor does it contain dry statutes, ordinances and testimonies. Its character belongs to the realm of preaching and teaching rather than of legalistic prescriptions. Although this initial written canon gives the impression of an ordinary book written in the form of a legalistic command, its profound dimension is that of an appeal to faith.

... he gave us this land (6:23). In addition to understanding the abundant love of God as a concrete historical action, as liberation from slavery of Egypt, Deuteronomy understands God's relation to God's chosen people in terms of the gift of the land. More than in any other pentateuchal or hexateuchal tradition, it understands the promise to the patriarchs and their descendants primarily as a prosperous and peaceful life in the land that God had already promised to the fathers (cf. 1:8-35; 6:10-23; 9:5; 10:11; 11:8-21; 19:8; 26:3; 28:11; 30:20; 31:20). God's blessings to his people are therefore not only spiritual but also material, of this world. This is why the land given by God to his people is constantly characterized as a land "flowing with milk and honey" and is compared with paradise (6:3; 11:9; 26:9; 27:3; 31:20).

Above all, it is a place of "good" (a *terminus technicus* in Deuteronomy, cf. 8:7-10) and a place of "rest" (3:20; 25:19), which Israel never owns for itself because God is the land's only owner. In fact, Israel in its entirety is owned by God; it is a people of God's own possession. According to Deuteronomy, the Israelites "are a people holy to the Lord your God; the Lord your God has chosen you out of all the peoples on earth to be his people, his treasured possession" (7:6, cf. 14:2). In fact, only in Deuteronomy do we find the concept of a "holy people" rather than that of a "holy nation" (cf. Ex 19:6). The concept of peoplehood was the basic idea of Israel's self-understanding in the Old Testament, but so it was also for the church (the "new Israel") in the New Testament. An examination of both Old and New Testament terminology makes this quite clear. The chosen people of God were an *am* (Hebrew), whereas the nations of the outside world were designated by the Hebrew term *goyim* (cf. Acts 15:14: "God first looked favourably on the Gentiles, to take from among them a people for his name.") This consciousness that when God made his covenant he created a "people" rather than a "nation", and when Christ created his church (the "new covenant") he created a "people" rather than a religious organization or a religious club, characterizes actually the quintessence of Christian mission. A wandering community in the wilderness in the old days, and an eschatological eucharistic community going forth in mission in the Christian era, the church proclaims the wholeness and the newness of the promise of the kingdom of God – not in the form of various world missions but as a single mission facing all aspects of human and cosmic life, witnessing the good news to all situations: geographic, social, political, cultural, economic etc. As the true manifestation of the kingdom of God, the people of God are continuously facing (to be honest, must be facing) all the harsh realities in the world.

The Lord our God commanded us... (6:24). Apart from a clear description of God's action in history, his love and grace for the world through his chosen people (redemption, liberation, election, guidance of his people in the Old Testament, and in the same line also incarnation and sending of the Holy Spirit in the New Testament), the biblical texts repeatedly emphasize that God's people are obliged to respond to the divine love and appropriate it for themselves. In Deuteronomy the response of the people of God is specified as obedience to the will of God and reverence for his name. According to our text, the Israelites in response to what God had done for them in history must obey all the laws and have reverence for the Lord their God.

... to observe all these statutes (6:24). We have pointed out above that obedience to the laws is not to be understood legalistically; they are not to be understood even religiously, or at least only and purely religiously. Faithfulness and obedience to God and to his laws are in fact an expression of love in return for God's love, and therefore have also social connotations. For this reason the laws in Deuteronomy, but also in the rest of the Pentateuch, cover a wider area in Israel's social life and refer among other things to the devotion between husband and wife (Deut 21:15-16), citizen and sojourner (10:19) etc. But nowhere is the exercise of love within society more evident in Deuteronomy than in the regulations concerning the poor and the slaves. The society promised by God to his people is a society in which "there shall be no poor" (15:4), and towards that fulfilment, and having that in mind, all people who in the meantime are poor or in need must be helped. It was exactly for this reason that when the problem of poverty became more acute and the gap between the rich and the poor increased dangerously, "the year of release", which originally applied only to the land, was extended also in Deuteronomy to the remission of debts (15:1-18).

Similar provisions were made for the slaves. Foreign slaves who escaped or ran away should not be sent back to their former masters; they should be allowed to live in any Israelite place of their choice and should be treated properly (23:15-16). Even more remarkable is the deuteronomistic treatment of the Hebrew slaves (15:12-18, compared with the same regulations in Ex. 21:1-11): they should not only be set free in the seventh year but also be given liberal gifts of food (sheep, grain, wine) and be sent away gladly for their six years of service.

... and to fear him (6:24). The main objective, however, of Deuteronomy's laws is undoubtedly to lead God's people to remain faithful to their God and to his covenant; in other words to respect and revere God. To that end the authors of Deuteronomy strive for a return to the pure worship of God at the one sanctuary in Jerusalem, reminding Israel that Yahweh, their God, is a "jealous God" (4:24; 5:9; 6:15; 29:20; 32:16-21). But this return is understood in Deuteronomy as a threefold logical process.

Israel, first of all, must put its unquestioning *trust* in God's divine plan for it. The people of God must never express fear or doubt about his purposes or his willingness to guide them to a prosperous and fertile land and to offer them abundant life; they must never despair or murmur, as they have done in the wilderness (1:27-28). Moses before his death "summoned Joshua and said to him in the sight of all Israel: 'Be strong and bold... It is the Lord who goes before you... he will not fail you or forsake you. Do not fear or be dismayed'" (31:7-8). This confidence and trust in God, which Israel must show in all situations, is not an unfounded or abstract one but is based on past history.

Second, the people of God must therefore *remember* all his actions for them. They must remember not only their slavery in Egypt (6:21; 16:12; 24:22) and their deliverance in the exodus (6:23; 7:18; 15:15; 24:18), not only the covenant at Horeb (4:9-23) or their experiences in the wilderness (8:2; 9:7; 24:9), but all "the days of old" (32:7). This remembrance, however, is not just a recalling of past history. It is a conscious living of God's presence in history, a manifestation of God's past action in the present. It was for this reason that the expression "this day" or "today" is constantly emphasized in Deuteronomy (cf. also 1:39; 2:18-25; 4:20ff.; 5:1ff.; 6:6; 7:11; 8:11-20; 10:15; 11:2-32, etc.).

Third, the area in which the past for the people of God becomes present, and Israel's trust and remembrance of God's loving action are realized, is undoubtedly the area of *worship*. According to the book of Deuteronomy, it is in worship that the reality of God's presence in history is profoundly lived, and in worship Israel feels in fellowship with him. It has been rightly stated that Deuteronomy pictures Israel, God's chosen people, as a charismatic worshiping community, and in this respect it foreshadows the true character of the church. Both Israel and the church are in fact liturgical religions; for both, worship comes first, doctrine and discipline, law and commands (even if this last statement sounds a little bit strange to Judaism) come second. Nevertheless, we must always remember that in Israel, as well as in the church, worship is never related to the very essence of God in an abstract way but to his concrete actions in history. In other words, the worshiper communicates with God through the medium of history.

... obey diligently everything that God has commanded us (6:25). God's will for Israel is inextricably bound with – in fact it stands as a consequence to – the covenant, one that God in his initiative made with his chosen people. Hence the idea not only of a jealous God, but also of the centralization of worship, which is emphasized throughout the book of Deuteronomy and which aims no doubt at restraining God's people from worshiping other deities. (Cf. the repeated command not to "follow other gods" [6:14; 8:19; 11:28; 13:2 etc.] or the reminder not to "serve other gods" [7:4; 11:16; 13:2-18 etc.])

It is not accidental that in the New Testament God's will for the new Israel, the church, is closely related to God's new covenant, God's kingdom. In the Lord's prayer the petition "Your will be done" follows – in fact is the consequence of – the previous fundamental petition "Your kingdom come." God's will for his people is therefore conditioned by the realization and manifestation of the kingdom of God, this "new heaven and new earth". And for Christian mission and the church, as the eschatological eucharistic community, there is no other will of God than the coming of his kingdom "everywhere on earth, so that error may be destroyed, and truth implanted, and all wickedness cast out, and virtue return, and no difference in this respect be henceforth between heaven and earth", as John Chrysostom so beautifully commented on the Lord's prayer, connecting God's will with God's kingdom.

8. St Luke's Legacy
for the Church's Mission

About 800 people from all over the world, representing different Christian traditions, gathered in May 1989 in San Antonio, Texas, USA, for the World Mission Conference of the WCC, aware that in the long process of the ecumenical movement their meeting was placed in between two major events: the previous World Mission Conference at Melbourne, Australia (1980), and the forthcoming Assembly of WCC at Canberra, also in Australia (1991). The San Antonio conference came in between the "kingdom of God" issue (Melbourne) and the church's constant cry: "Come, Holy Spirit – renew the whole creation" (Canberra). During the ten days of this great missionary event (22-31 May), the participants reflected in small groups on the Bible, in an effort to understand more profoundly the contemporary demands of Christian mission in Christ's way. Through this daily reflection on the most precious Christian heritage, the participants of the conference were in some way affirming that the ecumenical community, despite its commitment to an open and sincere dialogue with peoples of other faiths and ideologies as well as to common action with them, remained faithful to the common source of the Christian faith. What follows is my short presentation on the Lucan theology from an exegetical perspective for the Bible-study section of the conference.

The gospel of Luke was chosen as the most appropriate piece of biblical material for an overall presentation and coverage of Christ's mission, i.e. his incarnation, life, ministry, passion, death and resurrection. And to some extent the choice was successful, since the gospel of Luke can be considered as the missionary gospel of the church. It is a gospel most probably written for Christians of Gentile background one or two decades before the end of the first century. There is an old tradition,

• This chapter is an adapted version of remarks given in 1989 at the San Antonio world conference on mission and evangelism. An earlier version appeared in *Deltion Biblikon Meleton*, 9, 1990, pp.5-9, and is reprinted here by permission of the publisher.

going back to Irenaeus and accepted by Gregory of Nazianzus and Jerome, which in addition gives the gospel a Gentile place of origin (southern Greece). Even its author – "Luke, the beloved physician" (Col. 4:14), a man who accompanied Paul throughout most of his missionary activity – was of Gentile background (cf. Col. 4:11ff.). Luke more clearly than the other gospels stresses the action of evangelization (with one exception, all occurrences in the gospels of the relevant verb, *euaggelizesthai*, are in Luke), and this is the lesson we learn from the theological insights of its inspired writer. Five isolated texts have been chosen, which include different styles – a hymn (Magnificat 1:38-55), Jesus' preaching (beatitudes, 6:17-26), a parable (great banquet, 14:12-24) and two passages dealing with the life of Jesus in his suffering (Gethsemane, 22:39-46) and resurrection (Emmaus, 24:13-34) – plus a further set of verses (10:1,17; 8:11-15). Trying hard to renew our understanding of mission and nurture our faith and vision, we viewed these texts not as isolated passages but mainly as windows through which we could reflect on the entire theology of Luke. In fact, we turned to the gospel of Luke to answer such vital questions as:

– How did Jesus discover God's will, and how did he submit himself to it?
– What are the demands of following, or the costs of obeying, God's will?
– How did Jesus identify his mission?
– What are the demands and risks of doing mission in Christ's way?

Our Bible reflections, closely connected with the morning ecumenical worship (though not to the extent some of us would have wished), were primarily meant to build a community, not only among the participants but with the entire history of our undivided church. And for this reason, to this end, we were guided as far as possible by para. 45 of the ecumenical affirmation of the Montreal Faith and Order conference (1963):

> We can say that we exist as Christians by the Tradition of the Gospel (the *paradosis* of the *kerygma*) testified in Scripture, transmitted in and by the Church through the power of the Holy Spirit.

St Luke, writing as a historian, was in fact making an affirmation that the Christian faith is based on historical events, regarded as God's incarnational intervention in history. I need not belabour the consequences of this theology for the church as the body of Christ, in its incarnational participation in the suffering and struggles of the world. The core of

Lucan theology is the consideration of Jesus' ministry from baptism to ascension and the outpouring of the Holy Spirit at Pentecost as being accomplished in accordance with the divine plan of salvation of the entire creation (cf. Acts 2:23). That is why Luke repeatedly describes Jesus' ministry as a divine visit (cf. Luke 1:68,78; 7:16; 19:14 etc.). In the drama of the world salvation, people are free to act on their volition – they can even reject the gospel (e.g. Luke 7:30, many examples in Acts). At the end, however, God turns their rejection into victory. It is important to note that Luke makes provision for humanity to participate in the restoration of fallen creation in the person of Mary, the *Theotokos*, by her free will (cf. Luke 1:38). Without ignoring other fundamental theological aspects (soteriology etc.), Luke mainly focuses on the prophetic character of Jesus' ministry, thus showing an increased interest in Jesus as a human wonder-worker ("He went about doing good and healing all who were oppressed by the devil", Acts 10:38). His humanitarian rendering of the gospel was in fact designed to appeal to the average person of feeling. And this is what made his word the most effective of all, as a human and secular approach to the mystery of the divine economy.

Luke's gospel also reminds us of the *universality of salvation*, of how Jesus brought salvation to the Gentiles, especially to the despised Samaritans (Luke 9:52; 10:33; 17:11,16; Acts 1:8; 8:1-25; cf. Matt. 10:5) and to the less privileged people in Judea: to notorious sinners, to women, to children and above all to the poor (cf. the parable of the great banquet, Luke 14:16-24). For Luke this is the consequence of his conviction that God is above all the God of mercy, not of punishment. It also reminds us that our gospel is a *gospel of the poor and for the poor*. Right from the beginning in the infancy narratives, the poor and the lowly were chosen for the great privileges of witnessing and participating in the mystery of the divine incarnation: a childless couple, Zachariah and Elizabeth, Mary and Joseph from the unknown Nazareth, poor shepherds from the countryside. The Hymn of Mary (Magnificat) makes a strong reference to the poor and a renunciation of the rich. Also the beatitudes clearly affirm actual poverty, both by keeping the direct address of the second person ("blessed are you who are poor...", 6:20) and by avoiding mention of the "poor in spirit", cf. Matt. 5:3). Cf. also the exclusively Lucan material, which includes the full Isaianic text in 4:18 (cf. Luke 7:22 par.), the parable of the rich man and Lazarus (16:19-31) and the parable of the rich fool (12:13-21). It is also interesting to note that Luke has been characterized as a *gospel of women and for women*, not so much because of its contents, but mainly because it has provided the basis of the theological reflection in later times that Mary the *theotokos* in the divine economy of salvation represents the entire humanity. The *euagellion* (good news), as it is seen by Luke, is a *gospel of absolute self-denial*. The cost of discipleship is great (according to 5:11 the disciples must leave "everything", compared with Matt 4:18ff. and Mark 1:16ff.); the grace of God is not cheap grace. The kingdom of God is cause for total dedication: "No one who puts a hand to the plough and looks back is fit for the kingdom of God" (Luke 9:62). Luke adds even "wife" to the traditional list of what some will be asked to renounce for the sake of the kingdom (14:26; 18:29). In the third gospel we hear Jesus saying: "Sell your possessions, and give alms" (Luke 12:33), contrary to the Matthaean parallel text (Matt. 6:20). Yet the gospel of Luke is a *gospel of joy*, as its choice of *chara* and other Greek words shows. The messianic time of salvation inaugurated with Jesus' ministry, and continued in the church's ministry, is an era of joy, not of sorrow.

During those days in San Antonio we were also reminded that the gospel of Luke is the *gospel of prayer* par excellence and a constant reminder that Christianity is above all a liturgical religion. Worship comes first, doctrine and discipline second. The gospel begins in the temple (1:9) and ends in it (24:53), but gradually, after the split with Judaism in Acts, the form of worship is changed to a eucharistic gathering (Acts 2:42-47). Jesus is explicitly portrayed as praying before every important step of his messianic ministry: at his baptism (3:21), before the choice of the Twelve (i.e. the nucleus of the new Israel, 6:12), before Peter's confession (9:18), at his glorious transfiguration (9:28), before teaching the so-called Lord's prayer (11:1), in the garden of Gethsemane at the threshold of his martyrdom (22:41), and finally on the cross (23:46).

But above all what makes the gospel of Luke unique in Christian literature, in a way that has since determined the faith and the very existence of the church, is undoubtedly its understanding of the eschaton. Dissociating the kingdom of God both from the glorious moment of resurrection and from a specific historical event, like the fall of Jerusalem, St Luke enters deep into the mystery of salvation. The kingdom of God is no longer identified with an event that did or would occur suddenly out of the blue but is presented as a communion event: "The kingdom of God is among you" (Luke 17:21). The relationship, therefore, of Christ to the world and particularly to the church is seen in and through the Holy Spirit. That is why "blasphemy against the Holy Spirit" is unforgivable (cf. Luke 12:10). To deny the Son of Man may be due to a misunderstanding, but to deny the Holy Spirit as the divine manifestation of a new era, as God's inspiration and as communion, is to cut oneself off from reality, but at the same time from eternity. It is not an exaggeration to say that there is no greater contribution to the understanding of history, of religion, of the world or of the church than St Luke's further development of the trinitarian self-understanding of the early church – a development that reached its climax with the ecumenical definition of the dogma of the Holy Trinity. The implications of such an understanding of eschatology for mission can hardly escape our attention: the ultimate goal and the raison d'être of the church go far beyond denominational boundaries, beyond Christian culture, even beyond the religious sphere itself in the conventional sense. It is the manifestation of the kingdom of God, the projection of the inner dynamics of love and communion of the Holy Trinity into humanity, but also into cosmic realities. The lesson we learn from Luke is that true evangelism is not so much how to bring the nations into our religious "enclosure" but primarily how to "let" the Holy Spirit use both us, the evangelizers, and those to whom we bear witness to bring about the kingdom of God.

Reflecting on the gospel of Luke, one cannot escape the fact that the petition "Your will be done" is missing from the undoubtedly more original Lucan form of the Lord's prayer (11:2-4). But even in the Matthaean tradition this petition follows – in fact is conditioned by – the previous fundamental petition "Your kingdom come". God's will, therefore, is primarily identified with the manifestation of the kingdom of God. (Note that Jesus' prayer at Gethsemane, the profound meaning of which is indicated in the divine words "Your will be done", can hardly be other than the accomplishment of the divine plan on the cross, which in fact is the manifestation of the kingdom of God on earth.) And for Christian mission and the church as the eschatological eucharistic community, there can be no other will of God than the coming of his kingdom "everywhere on earth *[oikoumeñe]*, so that error may be destroyed, and truth implanted, and all wickedness cast out, and virtue return, and no difference in this respect be henceforth between heaven and earth" (John Chrysostom commenting on the Lord's prayer).

This understanding of eschatology by St Luke surely opens new dimensions for our churches in their passionate efforts to tackle the ecclesiological problem, which is of great importance in our ecumenical discussions. Luke, without removing the tension between history and eschatology, has shown us in a clear and indisputable manner that this fundamental issue is a matter not so much of church organization and structure as of eschatological orientation, something that has been for centuries kept alive (in some traditions more explicitly than in others) in the celebration of the eucharist, which is the mystery of communion, of love, and of sacrifice and sharing, but above all the mystery par excellence of the proleptic manifestation of God's kingdom on earth and a foretaste of it.

All these overtones of Luke's two-volume work have tremendous contemporary relevance. We all witness a scandalous contrast that exists between the affluent societies of the West and the North, and what is euphemistically called the "developing" world of the rest and surely of the East. We all realize also that poverty and underdevelopment are a direct consequence of the economic realities of the developed world. And we all realize that the individualistic and materialistic attitudes of the people of our day are a result of undermining – and in some cases even losing – all spiritual values. But at the same time we all witness a tension that exists in our missionary endeavours between theology and praxis, between worship and social action that sometimes destroys our holistic view of salvation, between the "already" and the "not yet" of the kingdom of God, between a glimpse of it we foretaste in the communion-event of the divine eucharist and its full manifestation at the second coming of Christ. The legacy of St Luke will remain always before the eyes of the church as a constant and challenging reminder as it continues to pray, "Your will be done."

9. Orthodoxy and Islam

Any dialogue among people from different religions is both delicate and extremely difficult. On the Christian side, ever since the 1938 ecumenical meeting at Tambaram, India, we have been rather consistently affirming that respectful dialogue with persons of other faiths is not only a necessity but in fact a Christian imperative, one made all the more urgent because of religious intolerance and fanaticism in all religions. (In this process, of course, we have no thought of compromising or relativizing our faith.) This conviction was reaffirmed in the 1989 World Mission Conference of the World Council of Churches in San Antonio, Texas, primarily through raising an anthropological issue. "The needs of humanity", it was stated, "are not divided among religions, but human need for life, for meaning, and for hope is surely one."[1]

All religions have as a basic mission, or at least as one of their main goals, the human person, the serving of humanity. This is true not only for those religions that proclaim that they have received the truth through divine revelation. It is particularly so for Christianity, which believes in the revelation of God himself in the person of Christ, as well as in the continuous presence of the Holy Spirit in the church and also, beyond her boundaries, in the entire humanity – in fact, in the whole created world. In posing the anthropological question, we in effect pose the theological question. Before doing so, however, we have to work on a rather more practical level. We live in a period of nationalistic outburst, which inevitably causes religious fanaticism. We therefore desperately need to reaffirm the necessity of bilateral interfaith dialogues.[2]

In this short communication, I am not going to present an account of the theological arguments for the necessity of such an interfaith dialogue (here, Christian-Muslim or Muslim-Christian). Quite a comprehensive

● This chapter is an adapted version of remarks given in 1990 at an Orthodox-Muslim symposium held in Athens. An earlier version appeared in Greek in the author's *Orthodoxy at the Crossroad*, EKO 4, Thessaloniki, 1992, pp. 191-203, and is reprinted here by permission of the publisher.

study is available from the Christian point of view by Anastasios Yannoulatos, under the title *Various Christian Approaches to the Other Religions: A Historical Outline* (1971). This outstanding Orthodox theologian and primate of the Albanian Orthodox Church here classifies systematically the expressed views on the issue into six basic theses, ranging from the complete rejection of all non-Christian religions to the radical view that Christianity does not have the exclusiveness of all truth, being just the first among sister religions. His very bold and honest conclusion is that the problem of interfaith theological dialogue is still unresolved and the whole issue is a theologoumenon, i.e. an issue that has not been settled but still needs further theological reflection.[3]

Almost ten years later, another Greek Orthodox theologian, Prof. Asterios Argyriou of Strasbourg, took the issue a step forward with regard to Christian-Muslim dialogue, calling for a new start of the theological dialogue between the parties, this time with the initiative of Orthodoxy, since "no other church has lived so close to Islam and has become so acquainted with the life and faith of Muslims as the Orthodox". According to Argyriou, there are "possibilities of a fresh dialogue between Christianity and Islam",[4] which can be based on more solid grounds today than in the past.[5] He therefore proceeded not only to a positive assessment of certain aspects of Islam, but also to a number of general theological grounds that such a dialogue can be based upon, including the eschatological character of salvation, the universality of God's covenant, the theory of the "spermatic logos" of the eastern Christian patristic tradition and the common mystical tradition.[6]

More recently, after I presented this report to the first International Symposium on Orthodoxy and Islam, organized by the Greek-Iranian syndesmos in Athens (17-19 December 1990), similar views were openly expressed in the Orthodox world. For example, the urgent necessity of a Christian-Muslim dialogue was stressed by Yannoulatos, who like Argyriou affirmed that "despite all theological differences and dramatic conflicts of the past Orthodox Christians and Muslims have, from different directions, reached a common cultural ground".[7] In addition, the Orthodox East, in comparison with the West, is better able to respond positively to the demand for a Christian-Muslim dialogue, partly because of the more advanced pneumatology of its theology.[8] Similarly S. Agouridis has stated radically that "the dialogue between Christianity and Islam has some possibility of success only if it has a realistic basis, i.e. if it asks the question what is truth and what is bias in each religion's understanding of the other."[9]

This brief report has a very limited aim. Leaving to the experts a more thorough treatment of such a delicate issue, it will only reaffirm its necessity by focusing on the two principal criteria of the Orthodox theology: the *liturgy* and the *Bible*. With none denying the significance and central place of the Bible, we first turn for a moment to the other pole of Orthodoxy, the liturgy, and remind ourselves that the very word "Orthodoxy" primarily means not "right opinion" (as it is usually interpreted in the West) but "right glory" – in other words, "right worship". In all ecumenical and interfaith theological debates the Orthodox thus insist that "Christianity is a liturgical religion. The church is first of all a worshiping community. Worship comes first, doctrine and discipline second."[10] In other words, Christianity cannot be reduced to a set of intellectual convictions (i.e. theoretical or doctrinal truths) and/or ethical principles. Rather, it is a communion of people, a loving and worshiping community of believers, that reflects the inner dynamics of communion and love that exists within the triune God. Liturgy indeed goes far beyond the ritual; it is, or should be, understood as an authentic expression of the people of God to the Creator, to humanity and to the entire cosmos.[11] In the eucharist, which is the heart of the Orthodox liturgy, the worshiping community offers its prayers not only for the sake of Christians but for the whole world; in fact, in the eucharist humanity acts as the priest of creation, offering or referring it *(anaphora)* to God and allowing it to become part of the body of Christ and thus survive eternally.[12]

At least two features, among so many others, are relevant to our subject: (1) the philanthropic language that prevails in all liturgical usage and (2) the trinitarian formula in the Orthodox liturgy (cf. "Glory be to the Father and to the Son and to the Holy Spirit"). The former continuously reminds the community that God is a lover of humankind and of all his creation; the latter points to the fact that God is, in his own self, a life of communion and his involvement in history (through the incarnation of Christ and the sending of the Holy Spirit) aims at drawing humanity and creation in general into this communion with God's very life. (In very simple terms, this is the meaning of the Orthodox teaching of "incarnation" and of *theosis*.)[13] It was this trinitarian and philanthropic understanding of the godhead that has kept Orthodoxy from imperialistic expansionism and from confessionalist attitudes. The Orthodox understanding of evangelism and of the church's mission is beyond these caricatures; true evangelism is not aiming at bringing the nations or the people of other faiths into our religious "enclosure" but seeks to "let" the Holy Spirit use both us and those to whom we bear witness to bring about the kingdom of God.[14] In Orthodoxy everything belongs to that kingdom, that new world and new reality. The church in the conventional sense does not administer all reality, as it was believed for centuries in Western Christianity; it only prepares the way to that kingdom.[15]

A further application of the trinitarian theology concerns the nature and structure of the church. By nature, the church cannot reflect the worldly image of a secular organization, which is based on power, domination, hierarchical structure etc. Rather, it reflects the kenotic image of the Holy Trinity, which is based on love and communion.[16] These points are crucial, because ever since the appearance of Islam as a world religion, there has been some misunderstanding, which eventually led to the enmity of the past between Christianity and Islam.[17]

Let us turn now to the Bible, specifically to the famous passage of the gospel of Matthew concerning the last judgment (25:31-46). It is not accidental that this passage in the Orthodox liturgical tradition has been placed at the outset of the most important and holy period of the church's life, the Great Lent.[18] It is also not accidental that in the gospel of Matthew this passage is set at the conclusion of Jesus' final discourse, which means that it was intended as the last word to his disciples. The scene of the story is an imaginative royal court in which God will judge the world at the end of history. One can paraphrase the story by saying that human beings are judged entirely on their behaviour towards their fellow human beings. What is significant here is that there is mention neither of faith as a presupposition of salvation nor of religious duties towards God. In fact, there is nothing about what we normally consider duties; we are judged on those things that we are accustomed not to consider duties, religious or otherwise. Plus in this passage all religious or confessional boundaries are dramatically brought down. We come face to face with the importance of humanity in all theological considerations in that God identifies himself not with any religious establishment but with those to whom service is given or refused.

> I was hungry and you gave me food, I was thirsty and you gave me something to drink, I was a stranger and you welcomed me, I was naked and you gave me clothing, I was sick and you took care of me, I was in prison and you visited me. (Matt. 25:35-36 and the opposite in vv. 42-43)

To their astonishment, the reply was:

> Just as you did it to one of the last of these who are members of my family, you did it for me. (v.40 and the opposite in v. 45)

* * *

These are, in a very few words, some of the criteria upon which a Christian-Muslim dialogue can be based, as viewed from an Orthodox Christian perspective. It is useful not only for humanistic purposes and for the interest of political stability and the welfare of our respective people.[19] It is also imperative for purely religious and theological reasons.

NOTES

[1] F.R. Wilson, ed., *The San Antonio Report. Your Will Be Done: Mission in Christ's Way*, Geneva, 1990, p.125.

[2] Rightly, therefore, the Ecumenical Patriarchate through its ecumenical centre in Chambésy, and in particular under the inspired leadership of Metropolitan of Switzerland Damaskinos Papandreou, has taken the initiative to launch regular bilateral dialogues between (Orthodox) Christianity and the other major religions, especially Judaism and Islam.

[3] A. Yannoulatos, *Various Christian Approaches to the Other Religions: A Historical Outline*, Athens, 1971, p.108.

[4] This is the title of Argyriou's public lecture to the faculty of theology of the University of Thessaloniki, published in their *Scholarly Annual*, 24, 1979, pp.381ff.

[5] *Ibid.*, p.403.

[6] *Ibid.*, pp.401ff.; cf. also his book *Coran et histoire*, Paris, 1984.

[7] "The Dialogue of Christians with Islam: An Orthodox Viewpoint" (in Greek), in *Anaphora: Studies in Memory of Metropolitan of Sardis Maximos, 1914-1986*, Geneva, vol. 1, 1989, p.227.

[8] *Ibid.*, p.230; cf. also "Orthodoxy and Ecumenism", ch. 2 above.

[9] S. Agouridis, *Visions and Reality: Questionings – Problems – Solutions in the Field of Theology and the Church* (in Greek), Athens, 1991, pp. 223-27. See especially his chapter "Christianity and Islam: Truth and Bias", pp.223ff., and "Greek Byzantine Bias about Islam: The Influence of National, Social and Cultural Factors", pp.162ff.

[10] G. Florovsky, "The Elements of Liturgy", in C. Patelos, ed, *The Orthodox Church in the Ecumenical Movement: Documents and Statements*, Geneva, 1978, pp.172-82, esp. p.172.

[11] More in "Orthodoxy and Ecumenism", ch. 2 above.

[12] J. Zizioulas, "The Mystery of the Church in Orthodox Tradition", *One in Christ*, 24, 1988, pp.294-303, esp. p.302.

[13] I. Bria, ed, *Go Forth in Peace*, WCC Mission Series, Geneva, 1986, p.3.

[14] More in "Mission and Proselytism", ch. 3 above.

[15] Cf. also my "Orthodox Theology Facing the 21st Century", *Greek Orthodox Theological Review*, 35, 1990, pp. 139-53.

[16] More in ch. 2 above.

[17] More on this in G. Ziakas, *History of Religions. II: Islam*, Thessaloniki, 1983; A. Yannoulatos, *Islam: Religio-historical Overview*, Athens, 1975; J. Meyendorff, "Byzantine Views of Islam", *Dumbarton Oaks Paper* 18, 1964, pp.115-32; E. Sdrakas, *The Polemics against Islam by the Byzantine Theologians*, Thessaloniki, 1961; E. Nikolakakis, *The Holy War of Islam "Jihad"*, Thessaloniki, 1989; etc.

[18] Cf. A. Schmemann, *Great Lent*, Crestwood, N.Y., 1974.

[19] So rightly Agouridis, "Christianity and Islam", p.227.

10. Orthodoxy and the Future of the WCC

An Assessment of the Orthodox Position on the Common Understanding and Vision

In my assessment of the Orthodox church's attitude towards ecumenism (see ch. 2 above), I have emphasized Orthodoxy's ecumenical commitment, despite some problems facing this church in recent times. Time and again it has been emphatically stressed that the Orthodox church should above all witness in the midst of the non-Orthodox its right vision of *communion* with the *other*, at a time when such communion with any other (and primarily the non-Orthodox) is becoming extremely difficult.[1] This means that the role of Orthodoxy in regard to the common ecumenical vision "is neither to proselytize, nor to impress and charm with its 'exotic' appearance; not even just to witness its tradition. Its role is to acquire and live communion with the other. This can only happen through a slow process, a 'kenotik' presence and a genuine integration. It can only happen in close and creative cooperation and truthful dialogue."[2] After all, dialogue is not only a means to achieve theological agreement; it is primarily and foremost an existential necessity, which is the most important and direct consequence of our trinitarian theology and eucharistic ecclesiology, issues for which the contribution of the Orthodox theology is widely recognized within the ecumenical movement. Konrad Raiser, in his book *Ecumenism in Transition: A Paradigm Shift in the Ecumenical Movement*, reflects on the crisis of ecumenism and suggests a radical shift in the ecumenical paradigm. One of the two key areas he addresses is the reassessment of the ecclesiological significance of the WCC, in particular because of the emerging new situation and the radical reorientation of the Roman Catholic Church with regard to ecumenism, after Vatican II, at least compared with its earlier exclusivistic attitude.[3]

When Raiser assumed his office as general secretary of the WCC, and after receiving positive signals from various Orthodox circles, he

---

● This chapter is an adapted version of remarks given in 1996 in Thessaloniki at an ecumenical symposium entitled "Common Ecumenical Vision".

asked the Orthodox Task Force to make suggestions in order to proceed with the convening of an Orthodox consultation in relation to the overall process called "Towards a Common Understanding and Vision of the WCC". The consultation was ultimately convened at the Orthodox Centre of the Ecumenical Patriarchate, Chambésy, Geneva (19-24 June 1995), with the aim of pointing to the way forward, reviewing the ecumenical commitment of the Orthodox churches and attempting to clarify underlying uncertainties in their relations with the WCC.[4] The official delegates of the Eastern and Oriental Orthodox churches of the WCC produced an agreed "background document" that contained some preliminary observations on the "Common Understanding and Vision of the WCC" reflection process.[5] This background document, which emphasized the ongoing character of the whole process, was submitted to the attention of our Orthodox churches for further reflection. One of the aims of the Society of Ecumenical Studies and Inter-Orthodox Relations and of this symposium coincides with this action.[6]

The aim of this short article is critically to assess this document, and at the same time to highlight some inconsistencies in our Orthodox official positions with regard to our ecumenical commitment, always on the basis of our generally agreed Orthodox theology.

The document clearly reaffirms the Orthodox church's participation in the ecumenical movement and in the WCC in particular, by repeating the expressed theological positions of the major inter-Orthodox documents (New Valaamo 1977, third preconciliar pan-Orthodox consultation 1986, message of the primates of the most holy Orthodox churches 1992 etc.). It clearly states that "the Orthodox church is involved in the WCC. because of its concern for the restoration of Christian unity. Our Lord prayed that his disciples be one so that the world may believe and the Father may be glorified. This prayer of the Lord is reflected in our daily prayer 'for the holy churches of God and for the union of all'.... Our involvement in the quest of Christian unity is inspired by the Holy Spirit. As St Paul has said: 'God was in Christ reconciling the world to himself, and he has given us the ministry of reconciliation' (2 Cor. 5:18)."[7]

When, however, the document addresses the positive results of our participation in the ecumenical movement, it is reduced to dealing with secondary rather than primary theological and macro-ecumenical aspects. It gives the impression that what is explicitly stated was for inner consumption,[8] not a responsible witness of Orthodoxy to worldwide Christian concerns. The Orthodox presence in the WCC is viewed as "profitable... [because] the Orthodox churches have been invited to give witness... to transcend all forms of isolation.... The WCC has served as a legitimate facilitator of meetings... among the Orthodox churches who, otherwise, may have been forced... to remain isolated from each other,... [helping] Orthodox theology to manifest itself in a fuller way... [and providing] through its resource sharing processes, human and material resources needed mainly for the development of the educational and diaconal services of the Orthodox churches".[9]

The crucial questions and challenges expressly raised by the main speakers of the Chambésy 1995 consultation, John Zizioulas, metropolitan of Pergamon, and Konrad Raiser, general secretary of the WCC, either remained unanswered or were rejected outright. The issues included (1) the so-called ecclesiological significance of the WCC, the possibility of establishing its "ecclesial character", with the inescapable concern to expand the ecclesiologically neutral character of the famous 1950 Toronto statement; (2) the concept of "one ecumenical movement", especially in view of the rapid developments in the Roman Catholic Church with regard to ecumenism, practised in local and regional contexts); and (3) the "movement dimension" of the WCC and the ecumenical movement in general – the "grassroots ecumenism", in R. Stephanopoulos's words, which suggests that not only the official established churches and their delegated representatives but the entire people of God participate in the ecumenical movement.

In his presentation Zizioulas argued correctly that "anything that contributes to the building up of the church or to the reception and fulfilment of the churches' life and unity bears an *ecclesiological significance*", observing that "in this respect, the ecumenical movement and the WCC are strongly qualified candidates". Furthermore, he made the straightforward suggestion that an ecclesial character – in the sense of the WCC being a "fellowship" through which the church's unity is being restored – "clearly belongs to the nature of the ecumenical movement and the WCC". Despite this detailed theological argumentation by Zizioulas, who made a clear distinction between "*being* a church and *bearing* ecclesiological significance",[10] the Eastern and Oriental Orthodox official delegations rejected the WCC's ecclesial character, making an uncritical reference to the Toronto statement.[11]

The issue at stake here, with regard to the Toronto statement, is that the Orthodox insist on its neutral ecclesiology, while they at the same time demand the expansion of the basis of the WCC to include a sacramental reference to baptism and to deepen its trinitarian dimension. Also since the Sofia consultation (1981) the Orthodox have denied participation in ecumenical functions to any Orthodox not part of the established hierarchy. Moreover, in all major meetings there is a statement and strong complaint about the thorny issue of proselytism. We seem to forget that the reason for not solving the problem of proselytism within the ecumenical movement after so many efforts and joint statements is primarily due to the Toronto statement! In addition to other factors,[12] it is mainly the neutral ecclesiology of the Toronto statement that allows every member church or Christian confession to have its own basic beliefs. (For some Protestant groups, a universal proselytizing mission constitutes the core of their doctrine).[13] But the Orthodox background document went even further: it implicitly denied the idea of the "movement dimension" of the WCC, stating, "We do not feel that the Council will be served by the inclusion of groups or movements."[14] It is inconsistent on the Orthodox part, on the one hand, to champion our eucharistic ecclesiology and, on the other, to deny participation as well as ecumenical commitment of the entire people of God. This is why all Orthodox, truly committed to the ecumenical vision of the church, normally remain outside the ecumenical deliberations. And those who are recently officially delegated are normally haunted by the ghost of the Ferrara-Florence council. In this way, the Orthodox contribution to the main ecumenical issues decreases, and a very poor Orthodox witness is maintained in the multilateral ecumenical dialogue.

What makes absolutely necessary a complete and thorough reconsideration of the Toronto statement in a more ecclesiological direction, however, are the new conditions, circumstances and developments within the Roman Catholic Church with regard to ecumenism, conditions not existing at the first stages of the formation of the WCC.[15] Here the Orthodox are faced with a real dilemma: either to follow the exclusivist position of the Catholic church and deny its formal participation in the WCC, or to participate in an ecumenical body but with full awareness of its ecclesial nature. And since the ecumenical movement cannot but be *one*, this must include the Catholic church too under the same umbrella. Otherwise the Orthodox will be in the very difficult position of having to deny the manifest logic of Roman Catholic ecumenical statements, like those expressed in *Ut Unum Sint* (1995).

NOTES

[1] In a paper entitled "Communion and Otherness", delivered at the eighth Orthodox congress in Western Europe, at Blankenberge, Belgium (29 October-1 November 1993), J. Zizioulas argued

that "individual Orthodox Christians may fail... but the church as a whole should not... When the 'other' is rejected on account of natural, sexual, racial, social, ethic or even moral – in other words contextual – differences, Orthodox witness is destroyed."

[2] *Ibid.*

[3] K. Raiser, *Ecumenism in Transition: A Paradigm Shift in the Ecumenical Movement*, Geneva, 1991 (translated with modifications from the German original *Ökumene im Übergang*, Munich, 1989; it has also been translated into Greek, pp.113ff. The other area Raiser addresses is the conciliar process for justice, peace and the integrity of creation (pp.117ff).

[4] For the proceedings of this inter-Orthodox consultation, cf. George Lemopoulos, ed., *The Ecumenical Movement, the Churches and the World Council of Churches: An Orthodox Contribution to the Reflection Process on "The Common Understanding and Vision of the WCC"*, Geneva, Syndesmos Poland, 1996.

[5] "Common Understanding and Vision of the WCC': Preliminary Observations on the Reflection Process. Final Document of the Consultation", in *ibid.*, pp.9-17.

[6] "With fear of God, our society humbly intervenes in this ongoing dialogue, although it is not only ignored by the local church; it is not even informed about it – on the basis at least of the fundamental theological principle of Orthodox conciliarity. Not to mention that it was for this reason, i.e. to assist Orthodoxy to the leading role it is called to play in the ecumenical dialogue, that this unique Orthodox theological forum was formed."

[7] "Common Understanding and Vision", pp.11-12, para. 11.

[8] By saying this, I do not by any means deny the need to resist the anti-ecumenical voices always raised against the Orthodox delegates to the ecumenical meetings.

[9] "Common Understanding and Vision", p. 13, para. 16-21.

[10] J. Zizioulas, "The Self-Understanding of the Orthodox and Their Participation in the Ecumenical Movement", in *The Ecumenical Movement*, p.45 (italics mine).

[11] "Guided by this affirmation of the Toronto statement, we do not view the WCC as a 'super church' (which is undeniable), nor do we ascribe any 'ecclesial character' to its being (which is questionable)" ("Common Understanding and Vision", p.12, para. 14). Cf. here the strong wording of Zizioulas's paper: "It was wise to begin with the ecclesiological 'laissez-faire' of Toronto but it would be *catastrophic* to end with it" ("The Self-Understanding of the Orthodox", p.42 (italics mine).

[12] More on this in "Mission and Proselytism", ch. 3 above.

[13] To be consistent with its outright condemnation of proselytism, Orthodoxy should abandon also any kind of similar activities in the West. There used to be a fine ethos, which is now fading away, not to consecrate for the diaspora Orthodox communities any bishop to a place belonging to the West, thus respecting the jurisdiction of the church of Rome, and consequently of Western Christianity, of the ancient undivided, holy, catholic church.

[14] "Common Understanding and Vision", p.12, para. 15.

[15] Cf. the insightful comments by K. Raiser, "Towards a Common Understanding and Vision of the WCC: Introductory Thoughts", in *The Ecumenical Movement*, pp.25-35; also his *Ecumenism in Transition*, pp.113ff.

11. Ecumenical Theological Education: Its Future and Viability

I was invited to reflect critically on Dr Raiser's keynote address to the global consultation on the viability of ecumenical theological education (ETE) held in Oslo, in August 1996. I accepted with satisfaction the invitation with the awareness that the viability of our theological education – particularly in its ecumenical dimension – definitely needs to be properly addressed. ETE's initiative to provide a forum where various insights and persons from around the globe will mutually critique, challenge and reaffirm the present state of ecumenical theological education, but also help clarify its task for the next years, has come at the right moment.

There is no doubt that the classical approach to theology is being questioned from various quarters at the end of this turbulent and division-prone second millennium. If some do not openly admit that it is in a certain crisis, very few would deny that it has at least run its course. Ever since the beginning of mediaeval scholasticism, and even after the Enlightenment, theology was defined as a discipline that uses the methods of Aristotelian logic. Rational knowledge was, and in some cases is still, considered as the only legitimate form of knowledge. *Theological education* thus gradually shifted away from its eucharistic/liturgical framework, in other words, away from its context in the local ecclesial community.[1]

The rational understanding of God and humanity had in fact led to a *knowledge-centred* and *mission-oriented* theological education. Most theological institutions around the globe have been structured in such a way as to educate church "leaders", not the entire people of God; to equip priests, pastors or missionaries with the necessary means to preserve and propagate certain Christian truths or ethical norms, and in

---

● An earlier version of this chapter appeared in J. Pobee, ed., *Towards Viable Theological Education*, Geneva, WCC, 1997, pp.66-72.

some cases even to defend old-fashioned institutions, not to build up local eucharistic communities.

They lost, in other words, the *community-centred* and *liturgically/eschatologically-oriented* dimension of theological education. Gradually, therefore, we all unconsciously lost sight of the most significant parameter that really makes theology viable: the often forgotten truth that theology is the real conscience of the living church; that theology is first and foremost the voice of the sometimes voiceless Christian community and one of its most fundamental tasks; even further, that theology is neither a discipline for young people at the end of adolescence nor a prerogative of professional clergy or academics, but the task of the entire Christian community, which is, according to the well-celebrated 1848 encyclical of the Orthodox patriarchs, the only guardian of the Christian faith. Consequently, little if any attention has been given to the fact that theological education is a worldwide enterprise fundamental to the mission of the church, not in its institutional character – the negative consequences of which have been sufficiently highlighted by Konrad Raiser – but in its eschatological awareness of being a glimpse and a foretaste of the kingdom of God, a proleptic manifestation of this ultimate reality that should always determine our approach to history.

Contextuality and Catholicity

This vision of the kingdom has unquestionably been reinforced in modern times through the ecumenical movement, which for a time created an unprecedented enthusiasm within a deeply divided Christianity that the centuries-long divisions of the church might find some sort of agreed solution. Unfortunately this momentum, which reached a climax in the 1960s especially through the historic event of Vatican II, did not have an equally optimistic follow-up. Ironically, ecumenical optimism and enthusiasm for the goal of the visible unity of the church was interrupted at the very point when an important achievement in the field of theological hermeneutics was reached: the affirmation at a world level, widely applied from the 1970s onwards, of the *contextual* character of theology. This great achievement has created an unbridged psychological gap between the traditional churches and the new and most vibrant younger Christian communities. The main reason for this unexpected and, at the same time, unfortunate development in the ecumenical movement was the complete negation of any stable point of reference, of all authentic criteria in the search for unity and ultimate truth in the post-Uppsala period culminating at Canberra.[2]

It is very significant that the discussions in this consultation will be conducted in the framework of *contextuality* and *catholicity*, and that the "ecumenical vision" is well rooted in the original planning in such a way as to direct our attention towards "how ministry and formation processes can further the unity of the church (John 17:21) for the sake of the unity and renewal of humankind and indeed all creation".

There is no question that it is impossible to make a case for the unity of the church while being indifferent to the unity of humankind. Today it is a common view in ecumenical circles that we can speak of "differing, but legitimate, interpretations of one and the same gospel" (Bristol 1967). It has become an axiom that "every text has a context", a context that is not merely something external to the text (such as theological position or theological tradition) that simply modifies it, but something that constitutes an integral part of it. None can any longer deny that all traditions are inseparably linked to specific historical, social, cultural, political, and even economic and psychological contexts. This means that the traditional data can no longer be used as a rationale for an abstract universal theology that carries absolute and unlimited authority. Finally, through contextuality, in contrast to the classical approach to theology, we are no longer concerned about whether and to what extent today's theological positions agree with the tradition, but about whether these positions have any dynamic reference and relation to contemporary conditions.[3]

Nevertheless, little if any attention has been given to work towards reconciling the two currents of modern ecumenism in order to soften the existing antithesis between contextuality and catholicity. I focus here on this extremely important dimension of the ecumenical vision, encouraged by the mandate of the organizers to work towards a synthesis of (1) the legitimacy of all contemporary local/contextual theologies and (2) the necessity – in fact it is an imperative, and not simply an option – of defining a core of the apostolic faith. It is my firm conviction that if ecumenical theological education is not only to survive but also to give life and lead to renewal, it must have a *common point of reference*. Otherwise, we run the danger of viewing *any* local context and experience as authentic expressions of our Christian faith.[4] Let me mention at this point the accurate observation by the late Nikos Nissiotis that we must not exclude the possibility of a universally and fully authoritative theology, perhaps even on the basis of the transcendent anthropology of contextual theology,[5] which suggests possibilities for making corrective adjustments to the contextual methodology.

The 1996 congress of the World Conference of Associations of Theological Institutions, held in Nairobi, Kenya (27 June-3 July), emphasized that the most important and necessary perspectives in contemporary theological education are catholicity[6] and contextuality: *catholicity*, in the sense of the search for a coherent ecumenical, global, and catholic awareness of the theological task; and *contextuality* as the unique expression of it in the various particular contexts. "Coherence" is important in that it expresses the authenticity and distinctiveness of different contextual theologies, as well as the need to bring these contextual theologies into inter-relationship with each other.

The task of achieving this coherent, ecumenical, global and catholic perspective is not easy. Central to doing so is not only the concept of dialogue, but also that of unity, i.e. the question of where the locus of Christian faith resides. In other words, without denying the contextual nature of theology, and taking full account of the indispensability of dialogue for the theological task, ecumenical theological education must answer the inescapable question: Wherein does the *unity* of Christian theology reside?

For Christian theology to seek a coherent, ecumenical, global perspective requires that no matter how many and varied its expressions, it must have a *common point of reference*, a unifying element that binds together all forms of ecumenical theological education and ministerial formation. It is necessary to focus upon the issue of unity in both general terms and in the specific ecclesiological use of the term as the ongoing quest to restore outwardly the given unity of the church. This includes consideration of the unifying and saving nature of the Christ-event, continually re-enacted through his body, the church, in the life-giving and communion-restoring Holy Spirit. After all, theological education is a worldwide enterprise fundamental to the mission of the church.

This given unity of the church, which does not necessarily imply a strictly uniform structure, is expressed in adherence to a broad understanding of Christian tradition. Such an understanding affirms not only the centrality of Christology but also the constitutive nature of pneumatology, i.e. the normative nature of a trinitarian understanding of Christian revelation. This trinitarian understanding affirms the ultimate goal of the divine economy, not only in terms of Christ becoming all in all both anthropologically (i.e. soteriologically) and cosmologically but also in terms of the Holy Spirit constituting authentic communion and restoring the union of all.

The communion God seeks and initiates is not only with the church in the conventional sense but with the whole cosmos. Thus the unity of divine revelation, as represented in the broad understanding of Christian tradition, is for the entire created world, not only for believers. This understanding challenges the distorted view that identifies unity with the maintenance of denominational loyalty, which in turn can be an exercise of oppression, excluding suffering people from the community of the people of God.

This understanding of unity in ecumenical theological education informs and challenges all expressions of contextual theology. It does not identify the unity inherent within Christian theology with any ecclesiastical or doctrinal system, and it recognizes the varied forms of human and social existence. In this way, it is congruent with the methodologies and goals of contextual theology. However, it also challenges these theologies in pointing out the indispensability of adherence to a broad understanding and acceptance of Christian tradition as that which gives expression to the given unity of the church.

Text and Context

In my view, the main reason that modern Christianity is unable to overcome the existing theological misunderstandings is the issue of the criteria of truth. And this is due to the inability to reconcile contextuality with the text/logos syndrome of modern Christian theology. It is time, I think, to distance ourselves as much as possible from the prevalent trend in modern scholarship of making texts dominant over experience, theology over ecclesiology, kerygma and mission over the eucharist. Many scholars cling to the dogma, imposed by the post-Enlightenment and post-Reformation hegemony over all scholarly theological outlook (and not only in the field of biblical scholarship or of Western and in particular Protestant theology), which can be summarized as follows: what constitutes the core of our Christian faith should be based exclusively on a certain *depositum fidei* – be it the Bible, the writings of the fathers, the canons and certain decisions of the councils, denominational declarations etc. Very rarely is there any serious reference to the eucharistic communion-event, which after all has been responsible for and produced this *depositum fidei*.

The ecclesiological problem, which is so important an issue in today's ecumenical discussions, is a matter not so much of church organization and structure as eschatological orientation. The whole Christian tradition from Jesus' preaching the coming of the kingdom of God, through the Ignatian concept of the church as a eucharistic community (with the bishop as the image of Christ), and down to the later Christian tradition (which understands the eucharist as *the* mystery of the church and not just one mystery among others) has emphasized the eschatological, not the hierarchical (episcopal, conciliar, congregational etc.), nature of the church.

Should we not remind ourselves that the church does not draw its identity from what it is, or from what was given to it as an institution, but from what it will be, i.e. from the eschaton? Should we not reaffirm our understanding of the church as portraying the kingdom of God on earth, in fact as being a glimpse or foretaste of the kingdom to come? After all, the main concern of all great theologians of the apostolic and post-apostolic periods was to maintain clearly the vision of that kingdom before the eyes of God's people. And the episcopo-*centric* (but by no means episcopo-*cratic*) structure of the church – the main stumbling block for the titanic effort towards the visible unity of the church – was an essential part of that vision. The bishop presiding in love in the eucharist is not a vicar or representative or ambassador of Christ but an image *(eikon)* of Christ. So with the rest of the ministries of the church: in their authentic expression they are not parallel to or given by Christ but are identical with those of Christ.[7] That is also why Christian theology and life should always refer to the resurrection. The church exists not because Christ died on the cross but because he is risen from the dead, thus becoming the *aparche* (first-fruits) of all humanity.

The importance of the eucharist and of "eucharistic theology" (more precisely of "eucharistic ecclesiology") in the ecumenical debate has only recently been rediscovered and realized. The proper understanding of the eucharist has been always a stumbling block in Christian theology and life, not only in the earliest Christian community, when the church had to struggle against a multitude of mystery cults, but also much later, even within the ecumenical era. In vain, distinguished theologians (mainly in the East) attempted to redefine Christian sacramental theology on the basis of trinitarian theology. Seen from a modern theological perspective, this was a desperate attempt to reject certain tendencies that overemphasized the importance of Christology at the expense of the importance of the role of the Holy Spirit. The theological issues of filioque and the epiclesis have no doubt been thoroughly discussed and great progress has been achieved in recent years through initiatives commonly undertaken by the WCC and the Roman Catholic Church. Their real consequences to the meaning of the sacramental theology of the church and consequently to theological education, however, have yet to be fully and systematically examined. Theological education should stop treating the church either as merely a cultic religion or as only a pro-claiming/confessing institution.

The eucharist has not been more successfully interpreted than through "trinitarian theology", i.e. not only as *the* mystery of church, but also as a projection of the inner dynamics (love, communion, equality, diaconia, sharing etc.) of the Holy Trinity into the world and cosmic real-ities. Ecumenical theological education and ministerial formation should therefore focus not so much on a doctrinal accommodation or on orga-nization and structure (faith and order) of the church(es) but on a dia-conal attitude and an eschatological orientation – in order words, on a *costly eucharistic vision.*

Education and Koinonia

With such a costly eucharistic vision, our future theological educa-tion can do more than develop gender sensitivity, articulate a new para-digm to equip the whole people of God and allow for an innovative, experimental, people-centred approach. It can also ensure that the processes of formation are relevant and renewing for individuals and communities of faith.

Theological education can no longer be conducted *in abstracto*, as if its object, God (cf. *theo-logia* = logos/word about God), were a solitary ultimate being. It should always refer to a *triune* God, the perfect expres-sion of communion, a direct result of the eucharistic eschatological experience – an experience directed towards the vision of the kingdom and centred on communion (koinonia), which includes justice, peace, abundance of life and respect for the created world.

What comes out of such an affirmation is self-evident: theological education should always refer to communion as an ultimate constitutive element of being. In other words, it should have relevance to the rela-tional dimension of life and therefore be in a continuous and dynamic dialogue, not only in the form of theological conversation among churches or Christian communities in order to promote the visible unity of the one body of Christ, but also with people of other faiths. After all, theological reflection on God's self-revelation to humankind can no longer be done from a christendom perspective.

NOTES

[1] Cf. also my article "The Future of Theological Education in Europe", in *Oikoumene and Theol-ogy: The 1993-95 Erasmus Lectures in Ecumenical Theology*, Thessaloniki, 1996, pp.11-24.

[2] More in ch. 2 above, "Orthodoxy and Ecumenism".

[3] It is a tragic irony that the 1971 meeting of the Faith and Order commission in Louvain almost led to a break because of the presidential address of the late Fr John Meyendorff, then moderator of the Faith and Order commission and one of the leading Orthodox ecumenists. And 20 years later, at the initiative of the Orthodox theological faculty of the University of Thessaloniki, an attempt was made to clarify the relationship between Orthodox theology and contextuality. More on this in my "Orthodoxie und kontextuelle Theologie," *Ökumenische Rundschau*, 42, 1993, pp. 452-60.

[4] Cf. Kuncheria Pathil, *Models in Ecumenical Dialogue: A Study of the Methodological Development in the Commission on "Faith and Order" of the World Council of Churches*, Bangalore, 1981, pp.393ff.; also Konrad Raiser, *Identität und Sozialität*, Munich, 1971; and *Ecumenism in Transition*, Geneva, 1991.

[5] Nikos Nissiotis, "Ecclesial Theology in Context", in Choan-Seng Song, ed., *Doing Theology Today*, Madras, 1976, minutes of the Bossey conferences, 101-24, p.124. Cf. also the special issue of *Study Encounter*, vol. 8, no. 3, 1972.

[6] Although the term used was "globalization", it was stressed that this very term can imply another form of domination, which would endanger the autonomy of the various contextual theologies.

[7] John Zizioulas, *Being as Communion: Studies in Personhood and the Church*, New York, 1985, p.163.